WORKING THE
LONDON
UNDERGROUND

WORKING THE
LONDON
UNDERGROUND
FROM 1863 TO 2013

BEN PEDROCHE

The
History
Press

Cover illustration: Underground tunnel construction work in progress at the Woodberry Grove site, north of Manor House Underground station, 1930 © TfL from the London Transport Museum collection

First published 2013

The History Press
The Mill, Brimscombe Port
Stroud, Gloucestershire, GL5 2QG
www.thehistorypress.co.uk

British Library Cataloguing in Publication Data.
A catalogue record for this book is available from the British Library.

ISBN 978 0 7524 9453 1

Typesetting and origination by The History Press
Printed in Great Britain

CONTENTS

INTRODUCTION

Stand on the platform at a busy London Underground station like Victoria or King's Cross St Pancras at rush hour and you'll see just how important the Tube is. Miles of subterranean tunnels form a network that keeps the city moving every day, with millions of Londoners and tourists depending on it to get them where they need to be.

With demand increasing every year, this is a transport system being crushed under the pressure of its own success. Delays, station closures and packed trains are a daily occurrence, causing much frustration to those who use the network every day. And yet use it we continue to do. It has become a London institution and an integral part of the life of anyone who lives and works in the nation's capital.

The situation isn't much better above ground anyway. London's roads are clogged with vans, buses and taxis, making what should be the shortest journey seem like a million miles. Trains are plentiful on the city's main-line rail network, but congestion on the lines in and out of major stations often leads to delays and cancellations here too.

Step back in time to Victorian London and the state of affairs on the roads was surprisingly much the same. By the mid-1850s the railways had arrived, allowing thousands of workers to travel into London every day for the first time. But rather than reach the busiest areas and the City of London, the railways instead created a network of lines around its fringes.

Travelling onwards into central London required the use of horse-drawn transport, which led to major congestion along every main artery in the expanding metropolis.

The solution was to go beneath the streets, and the first line on what would later become the London Underground opened in 1863 on a route from Paddington to Farringdon. Ridiculed by the press at first, a sceptical public quickly began to embrace the concept of descending into the depths of a centuries-old city. Soon thousands of people were using the new underground railway. It served its purpose in easing the congestion on the roads, and additional lines were soon opened in order to meet the new demand.

This was during a time when London's population was large, but nowhere close to the size of what the modern city has become. Step back to today, where more than 8 million people live in London, the problem has come full circle. The roads are full to the brim once again, but this time the problem is worse, because the great solution down below is also full to capacity.

It's an issue yet to be solved, but for now the London Underground continues to enjoy its well-deserved status as the world's most iconic transport system. It's one of London's most important assets, and at more than 150 years of age, it's truly one of the greatest engineering works of all time.

A large part of what makes the system great is the people that use it, and the journeys it takes them on. But most important of all are the people behind the scenes that make it all possible. It's these people that *Working the London Underground* aims to look at, as well as how the system was built, and how it is run.

The pioneering work of early companies like the Metropolitan Railway, whose engineers, architects and workmen constructed the original cut-and-cover lines in the nineteenth century, is explored first. This is followed by a look at how the first set of 'Tube' lines were built, as new construction methods allowed workers to burrow deeper than ever before, with more lines added over the course of the twentieth century.

The second half of the book uncovers the various jobs filled by some of the hundreds of workers needed to keep the system running. From the drivers who spend countless hours peering into dark and lonely tunnels, to the engineers dispatched to fix signal failures, it's an account of the many unsung heroes that have kept the system flowing for over a century and a half.

It's often rare to find people who love their job, but many of those working on the London Underground seem proud to be part of something so uniquely special. The fact that the original route is still in operation is also a testament to the dedication and foresight of the early Tube workers. They were no doubt aware that they were helping to write a new chapter in the long history of London, and it's a story that has since become an epic saga that shows no sign of coming to an end.

NOTES

The book focuses on how the London Underground was built and how it is run. The text therefore avoids lengthy histories of each line, and the formation of the companies involved. There are many fantastic books that cover such areas in greater detail, including several of the ones listed in the References and Further Reading section. Historical timelines also shift back and forth where appropriate, and archived photos are used even to illustrate some modern practices.

PART I

BUILDING THE LONDON UNDERGROUND

1

CONGESTION, CUTTINGS AND COVERS

The problem of congestion on London's streets in the mid-nineteenth century was the result of a huge swell in population, and the success of the City of London as the financial capital of the British Empire. The roads and passageways in and around the City were packed with commuters. The wealthier workers arrived via the various new railway terminus stations. The poor tended to live on the outskirts of the Square Mile, in some of London's most notorious Victorian slums.

The mainline railways had connected other parts of the country to London, but restrictions on building lines directly through the metropolis meant there was no way of travelling across central London and on to the City. London's first generation of commuters was therefore required to walk or use early forms of public transport such as horse-drawn cab. There were many different proposals put forward for how the problem could be solved. Many were frivolous, and almost all were outlandish. Ideas included a proposal by Joseph Paxton, engineer of the Crystal Palace, who designed plans for an elevated railway enclosed inside a glass arcade.

Another of the novelty ideas was an atmospheric-powered railway proposed in 1845 by a man named Charles Pearson. A solicitor by trade, Pearson had a vision that a new inner-city railway could have a far deeper social benefit for the people of London than simply providing a quicker way from A to B.

Building a new railway, Pearson argued, would mean that people would no longer need to live close to where they worked, in cramped and dirty streets. His proposal was to connect many of London's railway termini via a new line that would allow commuters to interchange between the two and therefore travel directly to their place of work from further afield. Building the railway would also be a chance to clear slum areas, as they would no longer be needed.

It was a noble idea, but one that failed to gain much interest. Investors could see the potential of connecting the mainline stations, but Pearson's social reforms held little sway with the profit-driven mentality of the moneymen. Railway building in central London would also be problematic, requiring huge disruption and heavy costs involved with having to buy land and offer compensation to property owners. It was for these reasons that parliament had previously passed legislation blocking any such railways, and that the mainline stations tended to merely circle the outskirts of the city.

Pearson was able to solve all such potential problems with his revised solution. He now proposed that his new railway should instead be constructed below ground. It was perhaps the most eccentric of all the proposals so far, but in fact made perfect sense. Building at the sub-surface level would avoid major disruption above ground, and therefore avoid the restrictions on building railways through the centre of London and in the City.

The concept again failed to gain investors, but Pearson was able to attract the attention of some of the mainline railway companies, who could see the potential for increasing their own passenger numbers.

After several years of appealing to investors, and the lengthy process involved in gaining the necessary powers, the new railway was finally approved in 1858. It was to be known as the Metropolitan Railway (MR), and would become the first of its type anywhere in the world.

CONSTRUCTING THE METROPOLITAN: THE WORLD'S FIRST UNDERGROUND RAILWAY

With the finances obtained and permission to build the railway officially granted, attention turned instead towards how exactly the world's first underground railway would be built. It was a radical new concept with

Underground railway pioneer Charles Pearson.
(©TfL from the London Transport Museum collection)

little in the way of any previous engineering project to learn from. Pearson's visionary plan for a sub-surface railway was innovative, but it would be nothing without a solid plan for how to design and construct it.

What was needed was an engineer capable of making it a reality, and the man selected for the job was Yorkshireman John Fowler. He had earned the respect of his peers through his work on several major railway construction projects across the country, but his employment in 1853 as chief engineer for the Metropolitan Railway was to be the defining achievement of his long and distinguished career.

Fowler was the driving force behind the decision to build the new railway using a method known as 'cut-and-cover', which had many distinct advantages. The basic concept was simple but effective. The railway would be constructed by digging up main roads, so that a trench could be built under them (the cut). The tracks would be laid inside the trenches, with the walls supported by brick. Once built, the trenches would then be roofed-over, and the road rebuilt on top (the cover). Stations would also be built along the route, either within the cuttings or above them.

Although there were genuine tunnels already in existence in London well before the 1860s (see later section), it was far from a perfected construction method. Cut-and-cover would mean that Fowler's railway would only need to go a shallow distance below the surface, without having to venture too deep into the underworld.

The biggest advantage of cut-and-cover was that the route of the railway could simply follow the direction of major roads, in particular parts of the New Road. Originally a turnpike opened in 1756 from Paddington to Moorgate; the section followed by the new railway is today the Marylebone Road and Euston Road.

Knowing that there would be nothing but a road above their chosen route allowed the railway to avoid having to purchase large areas of land in order to demolish existing buildings that would need to be cleared. It would be necessary for the route to leave the path of the New Road after King's Cross and on towards Farringdon, but it was still the most cost-effective method overall.

The next task was to tender contractors suitable to manage such a large job, and to deliver the construction on schedule and budget. The decision about whom to hire was left in the hands of John Parson, whom Fowler had made construction manager.

Metropolitan Railway engineer John Fowler. (©TfL from the London Transport Museum collection)

Two different companies were selected in 1859: the section from Paddington to Euston Square would be handled by a firm named Smith & Knight. The part of the route between Euston Square and Farringdon would be the responsibility of a contractor named John Jay.

A LIFE OF TOIL: THE HARD-WORKING NAVVIES

With the engineer in place, the cut-and-cover method opted for and the contractors hired, it was time to find the workers that would be needed to build London's first underground railway. It would be a mammoth task, demanding the use of hundreds if not thousands of men.

Fortunately for the owners of the Metropolitan Railway, there was a particular breed of labourer that could be relied upon for such a job; an infamous workforce usually referred to collectively as 'navvies'.

History tends to remember the great individuals who engineered the nation's railways, but the navvies have mostly been forgotten, despite the huge impact they had. They were a people with a long heritage of constructing the railway network across London and the whole of Britain, taking on the back-breaking work involved with laying miles of track, building bridges and tunnels, all while living with their entire families in squalid conditions.

The term 'navvy' derived from the word navigator, which itself was used to describe those who worked on navigable canals across the country, in the late eighteenth and early nineteenth centuries. Navvies had built the nation's canal system virtually by hand, including London's own Regent's Canal.

These huge gangs of men were willing to settle wherever there was work. Then, when the job was done, they would simply up sticks and move on to wherever else they were needed. It's estimated that more than 200,000 navvies worked across Britain in the nineteenth century, mostly agricultural labourers from Ireland and Scotland, or tin miners from rural Cornwall.

When the mainline railways arrived en masse in the 1840s, and with the work on the canal system largely complete, the navvies were able to serve the major railway companies as a ready-made workforce that could be used to construct their various new lines.

The appeal was obvious for both sides. For the navvies, railway construction was regular work and surprisingly well paid for the time. For the railway companies, the navvies satisfied a demand for huge amounts of manpower that could be exploited by the offer of a generous but still relatively cheap rate.

The navvies were also fearless, paying little regard to the common dangers involved with building a railway. The railway companies therefore didn't feel obliged to provide the men with accommodation, basic facilities or even safe working conditions. There would also be no compensation payouts for injuries or deaths suffered on the job. For the average hard-working navvy, the dangerous nature of the jobs they were employed to do was nothing more than an occupational hazard and a risk worth taking.

When time came for construction on the Metropolitan Railway to begin in 1860, the navvies were the perfect solution to how the company could go about completing the huge job of digging up London's roads and building a railway underneath them.

Taking into consideration the fact that this major new project involved the digging of long trenches through clay, it was a job that more closely resembled the canal work undertaken by the first generation of navvies than general railway construction work out in the open.

It would be perhaps naive to suggest, however, that these men were being employed for any specific expertise or engineering prowess. They were there for their brute force and determination for getting the job done. They would be building the new cut-and-cover trenches by hand, using nothing more than simple tools like pickaxes and shovels.

The only major downside a company faced when employing the navvies was the reputation that seemed to follow them around. If these were men that worked hard, then they played even harder, with tales of legendary sessions in local pubs that would usually result in drunken behaviour and fights.

It's likely that the navvies saw this as the only logical way in which to unwind after working all day in such dangerous circumstances, and the decent wage rate also gave them enough spare change to afford it. Whatever the justification, they would often cause havoc whenever they moved to a new area for work, and London didn't escape the mayhem.

In the three years it took to complete the first stretch of the Metropolitan Railway, hundreds of complaints were made to the press by local residents across the city. Later, when the Metropolitan District Railway (MDR) was being constructed, the navvies found themselves working their way through some of London's most affluent areas. Their presence and behaviour was no doubt the cause of much stress for the well-to-do residents of places such as Notting Hill and Kensington.

Work commenced on the 3½-mile railway in early 1860. The line would run from Paddington to Farringdon (named Farringdon Street on opening), with five stations along the way. Shafts were dug at Paddington, Gower Street (now Euston Square) and King's Cross between January and March. From here, the navvies were able to dig the trenches into which the railway line would sit. It was a labour-intensive task that involved hammering away at the London clay in conditions that were cold, wet and dark. Up to 2,000 navvies worked in two shifts, day and night.

Early construction work at Paddington. (©TfL from the London Transport Museum collection)

The building process itself involved bricklayers, carpenters, those skilled in working with metal, and various other roles. Contemporary illustrations show men working with the most basic of tools. The cuttings were dug completely by hand, with most of the clay and earth removed by wheelbarrow. Mechanical equipment was sparse, with the only real exception being a series of wooden cranes used for lifting timber, and a basic rig of pulleys that could assist with the removal of soil from the new cuttings. This could then be removed from the site by means of a basic temporary railway.

Away from the various construction sites, there were others hard at work elsewhere in London. There were millions of bricks to manufacture, and timber and iron to be prepared.

The cuttings were dug to a depth of around 16ft below ground. Once each new section of trench had been excavated, its sides were lined with three layers of brick. Timber and iron girders were then used to construct a roof over the cuttings, with extra thickness usually applied for sections of the line directly under roads. The cuttings were built to a width of approximately 28ft, as they needed to be wide enough to accommodate two tracks of mainline railway-sized rolling stock. As a result, even when covered over, the cuttings resembled rectangular boxes rather than the more genuine tunnels that would later come to define most of the Underground network.

In addition to the painstaking work of digging, lining and then covering the trenches, the navvies also had to manoeuvre their way through water mains and gas pipes almost everywhere they dug. Such obstacles often had to be moved and reconfigured entirely, adding delays and further expense to what was already shaping up to be a difficult job.

There was one particular section of the new railway that was required to be built as a conventional railway tunnel however, just after the route deviated from the New Road. King's Cross St Pancras Underground station is today located below the two mainline railway stations in its name. But the original station opened by the Metropolitan Railway was located further east, between what is now Gray's Inn Road and Pentonville Road/King's Cross Road.

Beyond the platforms, much of the new railway cutting was left uncovered, as it was not necessary for a road to be built on top. Just after, below what is now Wharton Street, the navvies constructed the 728-yard-long

Clerkenwell Tunnel. Although still built in much the same way as the cutting sections, existing buildings above it were maintained. This not only upped the ante for the workers in terms of danger, but also required some intricate design work from Fowler and his team of engineers.

In 1868, when this section of the railway was widened to allow for better interchange with various mainline railways (see later), the Clerkenwell Tunnel portal close to Farringdon was adapted to include a complicated gridiron structure that allowed the original line to run above two additional tracks after both sets had emerged from the tunnel.

The cut-and-cover method being used by the Metropolitan Railway in 1862. (©TfL from the London Transport Museum collection)

It's interesting to note that today Metropolitan, Hammersmith & City and Circle line trains travel through the original and now disused King's Cross Metropolitan Railway platforms. They are easy to spot from a passing train, and it's also possible to peer through a fence and down onto the platforms from St Chad's Place. More of the open cutting section can also be seen by looking over a brick wall on Swinton Street.

In today's workplace, where health and safety plays a frustrating but necessary part in our working lives, it's hard to imagine just how dangerous building the Underground network could often be for the thousands of men that made it.

History dictates that the navvies were a hardened bunch of men, but accidents were common, and there were several deaths during the three years it took for the Metropolitan Railway to be completed. One particularly horrific incident occurred just a few months into construction in 1860, when two men died as a result of a boiler explosion in one of the steam engines being used to haul wagons full of excavated earth.

Remarkably, there were no deaths at all in perhaps the worst accident during the entire project. Where the line veered away from the New Road after King's Cross, down towards Farringdon, the route instead followed the path of the Fleet Valley. It was formerly home to the infamous and highly polluted Fleet River, which was buried below ground as a primitive sewer in various different stages during the mid-eighteenth century. Working so close to the buried river meant that the workers had to be extra careful when digging cuttings in this area, especially as the new railway was set to cross the former river three times. Disaster struck in 1862 when the sewer walls burst open, causing considerable damage to the Metropolitan's works in Clerkenwell, creating setbacks and the need for much work to be recompleted. A section of the New Road also collapsed during construction, but workers managed to escape serious injury.

After almost three years of delays, financial struggles, accidents and backbreaking work, the new Metropolitan Railway was finally completed in December 1862. It opened for passenger use in January 1863 and was an immediate success, with more than 40,000 Londoners from every different social class experiencing this new Victorian curiosity on its opening day. Charles Pearson had died the previous year, and never got to see his pioneering railway in full service.

THE DISTRICT AND THE INNER CIRCLE RAILWAY

The cut-and-cover method of construction remained in use beyond completion of the first section of the Metropolitan Railway. The relative success of the Metropolitan had resulted in several similar railway proposals, and by 1864 a new company had arrived on the scene: the Metropolitan District Railway, referred to simply as the District.

The new company was granted powers to build a line on a route that would run from South Kensington in west London, to Westminster, in the heart of the capital. With the Metropolitan now having connected the mainline railway stations at Paddington, Euston (via the station at Gower Street) and King's Cross (plus St Pancras close by), the District would mirror it by connecting several major stations further south of central London. Victoria was to be included along the route of the first section, with later connections also planned for Charing Cross, Blackfriars and Cannon Street.

Crucially, the District had only been granted its official approval on the condition that their new line would eventually connect to the Metropolitan Railway at either end, in order to form an orbital route around the city with all of the mainline stations connected (Waterloo wasn't featured in the route, but would be connected to the growing Underground network in the years that followed – see later section). This was the origin of the Inner Circle railway, which would later become the Circle line.

Construction of the District began in 1867, in almost the exact same fashion as the Metropolitan Railway. Cut-and-cover techniques were again used, with John Fowler resuming the role of chief engineer. The same contractors were also retained, and the navvies were once again called into action.

The engineers and their hard-working men would face the same frustrations and dangers they encountered when building the Metropolitan, but this time there were also new challenges to contend with.

Although it was still considered the most efficient construction method at the time, cut-and-cover proved to be problematic during building work on the first section of the new railway. The Metropolitan Railway had had the luxury of being able to build its trench cuttings under an established road, but the route chosen by the District did not travel along the path of any existing road for long periods. The cuttings had to be built with various curves and bends instead, making it even more of a challenge for the navvies. It also required extensive demolition of buildings above the route, causing great expense for the company.

There were also additional obstacles that the navvies were forced to overcome. When work began on construction of the station at Sloane Square, it became apparent that the plot of land selected happened to stand in the path of the River Westbourne; one of London's lost rivers. Similar to the Fleet, the Westbourne had been driven below ground in the 1850s in order to allow for many of London's most affluent neighbourhoods to be developed. The only solution was to channel the river into a large pipe and suspend it above the station platforms. The original pipe can still be seen today.

Cut-and-cover trenches built for the District. (©TfL from the London Transport Museum collection)

Metropolitan District Railway construction site in 1869. (©TfL from the London Transport Museum collection)

The route towards Westminster would also mark the first time that any of the new sub-surface railways had come in such close proximity to many of London's most famous landmarks. The route was close to St James's Park, the Houses of Parliament, including Big Ben, and Westminster Abbey. The workers therefore needed to be more considerate than ever during the construction phase, and would have to take extra precautions to ensure no damage would be caused to such historic buildings.

The walls of the cuttings were lined with a thicker layer of brick than usual in order to reduce vibration, and extra ballast was also used to dampen the effects of trains running so close to the delicate buildings above. Over a century later, the workers tasked with building the Jubilee line extension would face the exact same obstacles, but this time with the latest advancements in tunnelling technology (see later section). But for the nineteenth-century navvies, it was a job that was successfully completed with only basic measuring equipment.

The next section of the District's new railway was completed by 1870, running from Westminster to Blackfriars. Its construction coincided with the completion of another great Victorian engineering marvel; London's new sewer system, designed by Joseph Bazalgette. The pioneering network of sewers included several new underground conduits being built along the north shore of the Thames. Once the sewer pipes had been built, they were to be covered over and a new major road built on top.

They were therefore being constructed using what was essentially the cut-and-cover method. It was logical then that the District railway should also feature in the plan, as it was to follow a similar path to Bazalgette's sewers.

The railway was built in an additional new cutting alongside the sewer. The navvies again had to be extremely precise with their work, and negotiate their way through an intricate network of smaller pipes and conduits that connected with the new main sewer. Adding to the complexity, the cutting along the sewer route also included two new stations being built along the way, at Charing Cross (later renamed Embankment) and Temple (opened as The Temple).

Steam outlet vent on the Victoria Embankment, above the original Metropolitan District Railway/Inner Circle. (Author)

On completion of the sewer project in early 1870, the new road and subsequent pleasure gardens became the Victoria Embankment. Finishing the railway had been a race against time for the workers of the District, as it was vital that their half of the project should finish at the same time as the sewer works. Financial struggles amongst the company's owners had delayed progress, however, and the railway had not been fully completed when the new embankment opened. Consequently, parts of the embankment structure had to be destroyed and rebuilt in order to allow the District's men the access they required to finish the job. The new section of the line and its two stations eventually opened in May 1870.

Throughout the construction of the District, the Metropolitan Railway had been extending their original route. The line reached Moorgate in the heart of the City of London in 1865 (opened as Moorgate Street), and much of the section of the railway between there and King's Cross was also enhanced in 1868 as part of a project known as the City Widened Lines (see later).

At the westerly end of the original line, the route was extended south from Paddington to South Kensington in 1868, where it connected with the District. The cut-and-cover method was again used to build each of the extension projects, although much of the route from Paddington to South Kensington was left with sections of open cutting.

With both railways now connected in west London – and the Metropolitan having then been extended beyond Moorgate to Aldgate by 1876, adding Liverpool Street to the list of mainline stations being connected along the way – the Inner Circle was edging ever closer to being finished. Having completed the section under the new Victoria Embankment, the navvies had pushed onwards with the new District route, and had reached Mansion House by 1871.

This left just a short section of the proposed circle unclosed. It was finally competed in 1884 when the two railways joined at Tower Hill. It was the end of a difficult twenty-year battle between the two railway companies. Fiercely competitive, the owners had fought continuously to succeed as London's biggest and best underground railway, and often used underhand tactics to try and sabotage their rival.

Even the completion of the Inner Circle itself was overshadowed somewhat by the Metropolitan Railway's dedication to undermining the District. They wanted to be the first of the two companies to build a

The curved platforms at Embankment station. (Author)

station at Tower Hill, where the two lines now joined. They ordered the navvies to build a makeshift station in just three days, which was named The Tower of London. A new, more permanent station named Mark Lane was later built for the actual opening of the Inner Circle in 1884, at which point The Tower of London was closed (Mark Lane station is also now disused, having been replaced by today's Tower Hill station in 1967).

For the navvies, the haste with which they had successfully built The Tower of London station was further tribute to their skill and hard work under extreme pressure, even when the pressure had stemmed from the rather childish antics of their employers.

Completion of the Inner Circle had been another difficult and arduous task for the navvies, but it was now time to move on. Millions of Londoners were now using the underground railways, and it was slowly but surely beginning to look like a network. There was consequently still plenty of hard labour to come.

TALES FROM THE UNDERWORLD

It's no surprise that a railway as old as the London Underground has its fair share of ghost stories. One of the many strange and fantastical stories involves sightings of a nineteenth-century worker walking along some of the oldest sections on the entire system. The narrative is usually tied in with a death having occurred at a station close by. As with most tall tales such as this, the details of the story tend to change depending on who is telling it.

BRANCHING OUT

The Metropolitan had also extended their railway further west a few years earlier in 1864, this time in partnership with the Great Western Railway (GWR). It was a new line that branched off at Paddington – a station that the GWR had built – and ran to Hammersmith. It was known as the Hammersmith & City Railway (H&CR), and would mark the first time that the Metropolitan Railway would venture outwards from central London, and fully out of the subterranean depths.

In complete contrast to what had come before, the line was in fact built way above ground, on a new viaduct 20ft high. Its construction was closer therefore to how mainline railways had been built across the city. With much experience to draw from, including the incredible London Bridge–Greenwich Viaduct completed in 1836, the new line was built with little complication. Although no longer part of the Metropolitan line today, the route from Hammersmith to Paddington now forms part of both the Hammersmith & City and Circle lines.

The Metropolitan also extended north of central London in 1868 with a new sub-surface line that ran from Baker Street to Swiss Cottage, and further to Finchley Road by 1879. Named the Metropolitan & St John's Wood Railway, it was built using the cut-and-cover method, but also shared some similarities with the deep-level tube tunnels that would come later.

The Metropolitan and District railways had been built to allow trains to run side by side in cuttings wide enough to accommodate two tracks. But the new line to Swiss Cottage had been constructed in the first instance as a single-bore tunnel, only able to accommodate a single track. A second tunnel was added later, creating two separate bores where trains were not always visible to others that passed by.

It was a short extension for now, but it would later become the gateway through which the Metropolitan Railway would change the face of London forever. From Finchley Road, the company was later able to branch out, with several different lines that would eventually run far beyond the borders of central London. It was along these extensions that the company was able to create the fabled 'Metroland', creating new suburbs in Greater London and deeper into Buckinghamshire, Middlesex and Hertfordshire. Thousands of new homes were built, encouraging men and women to use the railway for commuting into London for work and for exploring the city at the weekend.

Similar to the Hammersmith & City Railway, each new Metropolitan extension brought the company further out into the open and away from the darkness of cut-and-cover. In fact, they were now constructing railways in what was largely open countryside, with the aim being to develop new towns around each station they built. As noted earlier, it made the

Tunnel portals at Finchley Road, from where the Metropolitan Railway branched out to create 'Metroland'. (Author)

actual building of the new extensions a process far more in common with how mainline railways were constructed, with none of the problems associated with subterranean lines. It did present some new challenges, however, for both the company's engineers and the hundreds of men they employed.

On the extensions that would eventually run all the way to Brill and Verney Junction in rural Buckinghamshire, acquired by the company from existing railways in a period between 1891–1903, the men had to contend with working on a railway that ran through parts of the Chiltern Hills. The work may have only required upgrades and new stations to existing lines, but it was at the complete opposite end of the spectrum to the sub-surface depths they had been used to. The section of the line near Amersham, for instance, reaches heights of almost 495ft above sea level. There were also long stretches of wild countryside to navigate through, including the longest stretch between any two stations on the entire network; the 3.91-mile journey from Chesham to Chalfont & Latimer.

Elsewhere, the District was also extending its reach, first to Richmond in 1877 and then to Wimbledon in 1889. The new extensions meant that for the first time the District would be crossing the Thames. In the case of Richmond, the company was able to use the existing Kew Railway Bridge, built by the London & South Western Railway (L&SWR) in 1869 to a design by William Robert Galbraith.

For the line towards Wimbledon, the District worked in conjunction with the L&SWR to build a new bridge between the stations at East Putney and Putney Bridge. Named Fulham Railway Bridge, it was designed by William Jacomb, who had previously studied under the tutelage of Isambard Kingdom Brunel. Railway bridge building was nothing new in London by the latter part of the nineteenth century, but it was a new concept for those who worked on building the District. Today the Underground network passes underneath the Thames via several different tunnels, but the two bridges of the District line are still the only examples of where it crosses above it.

The engineering and construction challenges that had been faced by the builders of the Metropolitan and District extension railways would also be faced again by new lines that appeared in the decades that followed. From new viaducts and bridges over canals, to steep gradients and complex junction work, there would be many obstacles for the men building the lines that would later become the Piccadilly, Northern and Central. For now, though, it was time for construction to return to the depths of central London.

2

GOING DEEPER: TUNNELLING THE FIRST TUBE RAILWAYS

The cut-and-cover method used to construct the first underground railways had helped to revolutionise the way that people moved around London. It had many advantages as a construction method, but it was also fundamentally flawed for several different reasons.

The concept of digging up major roads was a costly exercise that often required complex parliamentary bills, and permission from various different London councils and boroughs. Once the necessary powers to carry out such work had been obtained, the work itself was also troublesome.

Having to dig up large stretches of road – including several of the busiest in and around central London – led to even more chaos on the streets. It was a necessary means to an end, but the extra disruption and congestion it created was a source of frustration for thousands of commuters and road users, and did nothing to persuade an already sceptical public that an underground railway would make their life easier.

For those with homes and businesses in Clerkenwell, the building of the Metropolitan had also turned their streets into a chaotic building site that was fraught with danger. Many also had to have their properties shored up with timber supports to minimise the risk of collapse from vibrations below. The work resulted in significant damage to several buildings, causing a long chain of compensation claims against the company. Most were legitimate, but many others were unfounded.

A further drain on revenue for the Metropolitan Railway and the District were the various costs related to the buildings they were required to purchase in order to make way for the new trenches they were constructing below the surface. For the most part, the route of the original line from Paddington to Farringdon benefitted from being able to follow the path of established roads on the surface (as discussed earlier, the route in particular was built just below much of what is now the Marylebone Road and Euston Road).

Inevitably however, there were instances where directional changes could not be avoided, demanding curves and sharp bends. This took the route away from the major roads, and therefore necessitated the clearing of any structure above ground that stood in its way. Several plots of land had to be purchased, often simply for the purpose of demolishing the buildings that stood on them. For the section above the Clerkenwell Tunnel, many buildings above did not require demolition, but the company was obliged to pay the landlords compensation for any damage that may have been caused.

In poorer areas, the cost of buying the land needed was often low. But later, when the cut-and-cover method was used again – this time during construction of the District and the extension of the Metropolitan towards South Kensington – purchasing land and property in affluent areas like Bayswater proved to be far more costly.

There was also a social impact to consider. The prospect of large-scale demolition in and around the Fleet Valley was sold to the public as a great way of clearing some of the worst slums in London. It suited some of Charles Pearson's own ideas, but in practice many poor families who lived in such areas had to leave their homes. The railway company was keen to downplay the number of people displaced and forced to move elsewhere, but unofficial figures put the actual number at as many as 12,000 people.

It's for these reasons that the cut-and-cover construction method was phased out towards the end of the nineteenth century. It was a decision that also coincided with advancements in technology that began to open up the possibility of expanding London's underground railways on a larger scale than ever before, using a new type of construction process that would solve many of the issues faced by the engineers of the original lines.

It was time to go deeper underground and create the world's first genuine 'tube' railway. Instead of running in simple trenches dug close to the surface, trains would now move inside tunnels for the first time, using principles learned from one of the greatest engineering works in history. It was a type of construction that would be refined and perfected in the decades that followed, and is still widely used across the world today.

BRUNEL, A SHIPWORM AND THE THAMES TUNNEL

In order to fully understand the new method of building underground railways that would soon come to replace cut-and-cover, it's necessary to go further back in time. Although his legacy is now eclipsed by that of his more successful son, Marc Brunel is still one of the most important men in the timeline of London's great history. By the early part of the nineteenth century, Brunel had found a degree of success with a number of inventions that helped to improve production across several industries related to the dockyards.

He had plans on a far grander scale, however, and turned his attention towards the concept of constructing a tunnel underneath the River Thames. It was an ambitious project on which to embark, and a somewhat ludicrous prospect to the casual observer. This was nineteenth-century London, however, where wild new engineering projects had become commonplace.

The challenge of building a tunnel under water was one that Brunel had originally planned to tackle in Russia, but in 1807 a similar project was already being attempted in London by another great innovator of the day, Richard Trevithick.

Born in Cornwall, Trevithick is today remembered mostly for developing the first steam engines and locomotives. He was also a skilled civil engineer and specialised in the construction of coal mines. It was a field that allowed him to gain much knowledge of how to work the material that lies beneath the surface of the earth, and he was drafted in to assist with a plan already under way to construct a tunnel under the Thames.

The project was set to become the first tunnel anywhere in the world to be built under a navigable river. It was to have a portal north of the river at Limehouse, and another south of the water at Rotherhithe, but by 1805 the original engineer employed to run the project was struggling to make it happen.

Trevithick introduced his own construction methods to the project, but regular and sometimes deadly floods forced the project to be abandoned for good in 1808. It was deemed to be an impossible task, but Brunel had quietly been developing his own ideas about how to make it a reality. His inspiration came not from any previous tunnel attempt, but instead from nature itself.

Brunel's time spent working in various dockyards had given him the chance to observe the peculiar behaviour of the shipworm – in particular its unique method of boring through wood. The creatures were a great source of frustration for shipping companies, but Brunel recognised the potential of applying some of their characteristics to the building of underground tunnels.

The shipworm is capable of using small but sharp, pincer-like body parts to work its way through the timber of a ship. The wood it excavates is then disposed of by being digested and excreted. The waste matter is then used as a way of strengthening the bore as the worm moves along, by lining its sides.

What Brunel took from his observations was key to the successful completion of the world's first tunnel under a river, and its basic principles have influenced the construction of every tunnel built across London since. The genius of the shipworm allowed Brunel to solve the two biggest problems that until this point had rendered man-made tunnels almost impossible: how to remove the earth being dug away, and how to keep the shaft from collapsing on top of the men building it.

By 1825 Brunel had acquired the requisite permission and financial backing to begin construction of his famed Thames Tunnel, connecting Rotherhithe and Wapping, on either side of the Thames. It was to be built using a revolutionary tunnelling shield of his own design, based on his study of the shipworm.

The shield consisted of a rectangular frame where up to thirty-six men could work at once, each contained inside their own section of the shield device. Each man was assigned a cell within the shield and was required to dig out his own section of the tunnel. As the tunnel progressed further and further under the Thames, the shield was propelled forward, and the tunnel walls were lined with brick in order to stop them from collapsing.

With no machinery yet capable of boring through London's infamous clay, this was a tunnel built by sheer brute force. For the men employed to work inside the tunnelling shield, it was a painstaking and arduous task that involved long hours inside dark, damp and cold conditions. It was also an extremely hostile and dangerous working environment, with the constant threat of danger quite literally hanging over the men's heads.

Fires from gas explosions were commonplace, and many suffered badly from the effects of noxious gases. Accounts from Brunel's personal diary during the construction of the tunnel tell of his men suffering from a wide range of illnesses, from vomiting and headaches, to more serious disorders such as typhus and blindness. Brunel himself suffered a stroke, and his son was injured on several occasions.

The biggest threat of all during any tunnel construction is the prospect of a major collapse. In the case of the Thames Tunnel, attempting to hold back the power of London's mighty river was often a losing battle. The project was affected by several floods, the most devastating of which occurred in January 1828, when six men were killed.

The dangers of a major flood didn't come solely with the risk of drowning either. The water that could come gushing in at any time was also full of human waste, the project coming as it did just before London was sanitised by the introduction of public sewers.

After eighteen years of delays, tragic accidents and financial ruin, the Thames Tunnel finally opened in 1843. It would prove to be a commercial failure, but from an engineering perspective it was the crowning achievement of Marc Brunel's career, and that of his son, Isambard Kingdom Brunel.

Although none of the blame for the tunnel's failure as a business venture could be placed upon the ordinary men who had worked so tirelessly to build it, it was no doubt still a crushing blow. Nevertheless, they had built one of the greatest achievements of the Victorian era, and one that would kick-start the long-term success of what would later become the London Underground.

The tunnel itself was in fact later sold for use by the city's railways, forming a section of a route that appeared on Tube maps as part of the Underground network from 1933–2007. It was listed for many years as a branch of the Metropolitan line and branded with the Met's familiar purple colour. It later became the self-contained East London line, boasting its own orange-coloured identity. Since 2010 the line has operated as part of the London Overground network, with trains still running through the Thames Tunnel today.

PETER WILLIAM BARLOW AND THE TOWER SUBWAY

Twenty-six years after the completion of the Thames Tunnel, yet another ambitious cross-river project was under way. This time the plan was to

The Thames Tunnel as it looks today. (Author)

construct a tunnel that would take passengers under the river via cable-operated carriages. It was known as the Tower Subway, and was constructed using new techniques that expanded upon the same basic concept of Marc Brunel's earlier tunnelling shield.

The man tasked with building the new tunnel was designer Peter William Barlow, whose primary concern was to build the new tunnel in a way that would avoid the same mistakes and mishaps suffered by Brunel. He improved upon Marc Brunel's rectangular tunnelling shield by opting instead for a circular design.

Today, our perception of a tunnel is almost always as being something with a circular design, in the shape of a 'tube'. Until the Tower Subway however, London's pioneering below-ground structures had all been wider. The Thames Tunnel was close to being circular, but the rectangular shield prevented it from being fully rounded. Meanwhile, the cut-and-cover trenches being built around the same time as the Tower Subway were large and rectangular in shape.

Assisting Barlow in the design of the new shield was his protégé, engineer James Henry Greathead. Again building on the earlier work of Marc Brunel, Greathead contributed several of his own innovations to Barlow's shield. Their combined efforts allowed for the Tower Subway to be completed in a mere fourteen weeks.

Portrait of James Henry Greathead. (©TfL from the London Transport Museum collection)

The basic principle of the shield was the same as Brunel's – men working by hand in their own section of the shield, with the entire device shifting forward by mechanical jacks as the tunnel progressed, and each new section shored up, this time with metal segments.

The speed was achieved as a result of the shield's circular shape, as a smaller diameter required less earth to be excavated. Crucially, the new tunnel had been built deeper than Brunel's, taking advantage of a harder level of clay that was less vulnerable to collapse.

The various shield enhancements not only improved the construction of the actual tunnel, but also the conditions for the men who built it (by now a team of workers generally referred to as miners rather than navvies). The smaller, circular shield required fewer men during a single shift, and the deeper level lessened the risk of flooding. It was still an unforgiving place to work, but less so than the Thames Tunnel.

Sharing a similar fate to the Brunel tunnel, the Tower Subway was a huge financial failure. It opened as the world's first truly underground railway in 1870, but closed later in the year. It was later converted for pedestrian use, although that too was a failure, as foot passengers much preferred to simply cross the river above ground via the newly opened Tower Bridge close by. The disused tunnel was then used as part of London's hydraulic power network, and is still used today for utility pipes and telecommunication wires.

SIBLING RIVALRY

Peter William Barlow wasn't the only member of the family with a flair for Victorian engineering. His brother was renowned designer William Henry Barlow, whose list of contributions to London's railway network includes St Pancras station. The awkward placement of the station called for precise engineering, and Barlow devised a solution involving the platforms being elevated above street level. The space below was used to store beer barrels delivered by train. The station was remodelled in the first decade of the twenty-first century, including restoration of Barlow's breathtaking train shed roof.

THE GREATHEAD SHIELD AND THE CITY & SOUTH LONDON RAILWAY

The legacy of the Tower Subway is in fact far greater than its current status would suggest. Its successful use of a new tunnelling method would soon inspire the next chapter in the development of the underground railways, resulting in huge expansion.

By the late 1870s, Greathead had become the leading engineer for various new railway companies each looking to venture underground. One company that Greathead was particularly involved with was the City of London & Southwark Subway, founded in 1883. It was created in order to build the world's first deep-level underground railway, on a route that would run from Southwark (Elephant and Castle to be exact) to the heart of the City of London.

It was to be built using the same construction techniques as the Tower Subway, with Greathead as chief engineer. He lobbied hard to generate interest in the new venture and was influential in helping the project to obtain the necessary Royal Assent in 1884. The scope of the project was then extended further before work even began, with a revised route that would run from King William Street, near Monument, to Stockwell in south-west London. It was to be officially known as the City & South London Railway (C&SLR), and it would be the start of a long process that would eventually change the city's transport network forever.

To use what by now had become widely known as the Greathead Shield to build a new underground railway made perfect sense from a practical perspective. It was faster and less disruptive, but its biggest advantage was that it allowed a company such as the C&SLR to get closer to the lucrative City than ever before, handing them guaranteed financial success.

The cut-and-cover lines of the Metropolitan Railway and Metropolitan District Railway had helped to significantly reduce congestion on the streets of London. It wasn't enough, however, and by the latter part of the nineteenth century the continual rise in population had only made the problem worse.

The most congested area of all was the City of London, a result of the shortcomings of London's rail infrastructure until this point. The mainline termini stations were well established, as indeed were the cut-and-cover lines. But the restrictions on building railways directly through the centre of London were largely still in place, and so the existing railways simply formed a circle around the centre. Commuters were still therefore required to continue their journey by other means of transport, thus creating chaos in central London once again.

The restrictions had in part been imposed as a way of ensuring that London's many historical roads, monuments and buildings would not be damaged by the heavy disruption that rail construction required. Therefore, if the long-term solution to London's congestion issues was in fact to continue to build below the surface, cut-and-cover would no longer be an option.

The key to the Tower Subway's largely trouble-free construction had been the decision to go deeper beneath the river than the Thames Tunnel. The new railway line being developed by Greathead would again require a new tunnel under the Thames and parts of the City, and this new technique of digging deeper than ever before was the crucial factor that swayed both financiers and Parliament to back the project. Constructing actual tunnels far below the surface would mean that no roads would need to be dug up. The depth also meant that damage to historical structures above was less likely.

Although based on the tunnelling shield that Greathead and Barlow had developed for the Tower Subway, the version used for construction of the C&SLR was in fact a new and greatly improved version. Amongst the new innovations added by Greathead were enhanced hydraulic jacks capable of pushing the shield forward quicker when each new section of the tunnel had been dug.

For the men working at the tunnel face, it was still a dark and dirty place to earn a living, but many of the dangers faced by the pioneers of the Thames Tunnel were no longer now an issue. The threat of floods or noxious gases from polluted water was non-existent during construction of the route on either side of the Thames. For the new crossing under the river itself, the techniques defined by the Tower Subway were further developed, ensuring a relatively safe workplace for the brave men tasked with digging the new tunnel.

The City & South London Railway also had another claim to fame that would make life easier for those who were employed to work the route. In addition to being the first deep-level railway anywhere in the world, it was also the first underground railway to be electrified.

A Greathead Shield section preserved at the London Transport Museum depot in Acton. (Author)

With the tunnels having been built so deep below the surface, it would have been impossible for smoke to be released in the same way as on the cut-and-cover lines. Steam-powered trains were therefore out of the question. The new railway would instead be powered by electricity, generated at the company's own small-scale power station at Stockwell (now demolished). Train drivers, guards and any other staff member spending prolonged periods in and around the platforms would therefore no longer be subjected to the harmful effects of sulphur and other chemicals, all of which had been a serious health concern for the workers of the Metropolitan and District.

The new railway was completed by 1890, and opened to the public in December of the same year. Its connection with the City made it an instant success as a commercial venture, with commuters now able to travel more easily through central London. Deep-level tunnelling had however been an expensive process.

Other than the original terminus station at King William Street, which closed in 1900, the City & South London Railway route is still in use today and now forms part of the Northern line.

James Henry Greathead memorial statue outside Bank station. (Author)

From an engineering perspective, it was now clear that deep-level underground lines were the logical way forward for London's subterranean railways. What Greathead had achieved would become the blueprint, and the success of his new City & South London Railway would soon be replicated across London, with a rush of new companies eager to build their own similar lines.

WATERLOO GETS ITS CONNECTION

By the end of the nineteenth century, the City was still seen as the key area of central London that the various railway companies were desperate to reach. Having opened in July 1848 by the London and South Western Railway, Waterloo railway station had by now become well established as one of the busiest in all of London. It was located on the south side of the Thames, but the original plan was that the station would provide interchange with through-services that would take passengers into the City.

Rising costs saw it open as a terminus station instead, which left City commuters facing the same issues experienced at the other great London termini; if they wished to travel to the City, they would need to complete the journey by other means.

Inspired by the success of the C&SLR, the L&SWR decided that the solution was to construct a new deep-level underground railway. It would link Waterloo with a new station at Bank, located in the heart of London's financial district. Use of the deep-level tunnelling method meant that the company could bypass the restrictions on building above-ground railways through central London, and therefore opting for a tunnel under the Thames made for a viable, albeit time-consuming solution.

It was to be known as the Waterloo & City Railway, and work began in 1894, with James Henry Greathead employed once again as principal engineer. This time, however, Greathead would also be working with William Robert Galbraith. Although perhaps not quite as well remembered today as many of his peers, Galbraith built several important railway structures during his time as in-house engineer for the London and South Western Railway, including Kew Railway Bridge and several viaducts still in use today.

The construction of the new railway came during a period of significant policy change relating to how new underground routes should be built. The City & South London Railway had been a success at least in engineering terms, but the decision to construct its tunnels to a relatively small diameter would later cause problems when the route was extended, and when better rolling stock was required. Lessons would need to be learnt before the next set of tube railways were started, and therefore new parliamentary legislation was passed in 1892 that outlined several new recommendations.

Underground rail tunnels were now required to be built to a diameter of at least 11ft. The Waterloo & City Railway project would therefore demand the use of an adapted, larger version of the Greathead Shield. With just two stations, one at either end, at Waterloo and Bank, the entire railway was to be a mere 1½ miles long. But a wider diameter, spread across the full length of the route, still amounted to considerable extra expense for the L&SWR, plus the additional manpower that it would demand.

Another change outlined in the new legislation was that it would no longer be necessary for railway companies to purchase land that they planned to tunnel under. Instead, all that was now required was simple planning permission. It was a crucial change that made underground tunnelling far more cost-effective. Better still, permission to tunnel underneath London's existing roads would now be granted for free. It allowed the L&SWR to make huge savings, but the decision to take advantage of the free access to road routes made the project an even greater challenge for the engineers.

Much of the short route is taken up by the stretch of tunnel under the Thames, and this section could therefore be constructed in a straight line, from one bank of the river to the other – much like the Thames Tunnel. Unlike the Thames Tunnel, however, where the structure ends when it reaches dry land at Wapping and Rotherhithe, the Waterloo & City Railway also required a section of running tunnel to connect the south bank of the river with Waterloo station, and another stretch north of the river to Bank station. To follow a straight line would also have been the easiest option here, but the prospect of being able to tunnel under roads for free was an offer too great to miss.

The result is that the non-river sections of the Waterloo & City Railway tunnels had to be built with several directional changes, making it a more troublesome and time-consuming endeavour for the miners sent below ground to build it. On the Waterloo side the route follows part of what is now Stamford Street, and on the Bank side much of the tunnel was built below Queen Victoria Street.

Similar to the railway tunnels that came before it, the Waterloo & City Railway was built completely by hand, with hundreds of miners picking away at the London clay, inside a Greathead Shield. A contemporary account from the weekly newspaper *The Graphic*, written in November 1895, gives some indication of what conditions were like for the men working in shifts, non-stop day and night. The age-old threat of flooding was a constant problem on the section of tunnel under the river. Instead of using pumps to expel water that would inevitably seep into the new tunnel, the engineers used compressed air to section-off parts of the shaft and remove water this way. It required a complex system of compression chambers, vaulted doors, pressure valves and warning signals; all of which no doubt created a daunting working environment.

The tunnel was completed in four years, and opened for business in 1893. The railway would spend most of its history under the ownership

Section of Greathead Shield embedded in a Waterloo & City passageway. (Author)

of the mainline railways, before finally becoming part of the London Underground network in 1994. It was rebranded soon after as the Waterloo & City line and given its own turquoise colour on the iconic London Underground map.

Part of the original Greathead Shield used to build the Waterloo & City Railway has been kept as a monument, and is now built into one of the passenger walkways at Bank station.

THE CITY WIDENED LINES AND THE GREAT NORTHERN & CITY RAILWAY

With the Waterloo & City Railway complete, the London and South Western Railway now had its own connection from their mainline station into the prized City of London. North of the Thames, meanwhile, another of the major railway companies was also aiming to achieve something similar.

The Great Northern Railway (GNR) had successfully arrived into central London via their terminus at King's Cross station, opened in October 1852. The company had then been able to extend their reach towards the City in 1868, thanks to a project that expanded the Metropolitan Railway, known as the City Widened Lines.

The original cut-and-cover route built by the Metropolitan had provided passengers with a connection to several mainline stations before terminating at Farringdon. When the company extended the line to Moorgate, an extra pair of tracks was constructed alongside the original two, with a view to allowing mainline railway companies to use them. A company such as the GNR would not only be able to offer their customers the option to interchange with the cut-and-cover underground railway at King's Cross, but also to continue their journey onwards on actual GNR trains, directly into the City.

Considering that almost all of the City Widened Lines route followed the original Metropolitan, they were again constructed using mostly the cut-and-cover method, with minimal disruption to buildings and roads above ground.

Despite a stormy relationship with the Metropolitan, the GNR found great success with their use of the extra lines, but in the space of just a few years the new route was beginning to contribute to a new problem. With mainline, suburban and City Widened Line services all now running through King's Cross, plus Midland Railway services via St Pancras also using the route, the lines were becoming congested from so much heavy traffic. It was starting to cause serious delays, in particular for those commuters heading for the City.

It was decided therefore that the Great Northern Railway would construct its own deep-level railway in 1898, as a way of easing congestion. This being a deep-level line, and the concept still being relatively new, with the City & South London Railway only having been opened eight years previously in 1890, the expertise of James Henry Greathead was called upon yet again.

Greathead had long been a supporter of the proposed Great Northern & City Railway, and had devised a route from the GNR's existing station at Finsbury Park, where trains could leave the mainline via a new tunnel. They could then run free of congestion through to Moorgate in the City.

The trains that were set to run the line were steam-operated. As discussed earlier, deep-level tube lines were not suitable for steam, as it was difficult to disperse the smoke they created. This therefore created a problem for the new tunnel route, but Greathead was able to suggest a solution that involved the trains being adapted to run on both steam and electric. The switch to electric would be made once the train entered the tunnel section at Drayton Park, allowing it to travel deep below the surface to Moorgate.

Construction work at King's Cross. (©TfL from the London Transport Museum collection)

Despite being customised for this purpose, the size and shape of the rolling stock did not change. The new tunnels therefore had to be constructed to a larger diameter than any of Greathead's previous designs. The new route thus stood out as being unique among London's deep-level railways, and as a result it gained a distinctive nickname. It may have officially been called the Great Northern & City Railway, but was widely referred to instead as simply the 'Big Tube'.

The actual techniques used to build the tunnel were much the same as those used for the construction of the C&SLR and Waterloo & City Railway. The Greathead method was deployed, albeit with an adapted version of the shield that could achieve the larger diameter tunnels. The new railway opened in 1904, although by now the Great Northern Railway had all but abandoned the project due to conflicts over construction costs.

The route was taken over by the Metropolitan in 1913. The fledging company planned to connect the Big Tube to other routes along the developing Underground system, but none of the plans came to fruition.

When the various underground railway companies later combined to form one network (see later), the route became part of the Northern line, but was transferred to the National Rail network in 1975. Passenger services still run through the Big Tube today, although its heritage as part of the London Underground has long since been forgotten.

EAST TO WEST:
BUILDING THE CENTRAL LONDON RAILWAY

Deep-level underground railways were now well established in London, but they had a major flaw. Construction costs tended to be huge, and therefore a railway company building one would need to be massively successful in order to recoup the costs and start to make a significant profit.

Despite its initial success, the City & South London Railway struggled to make money. Its commercial failure was thanks to a series of bad choices by the railway's owners, with everything from power to rolling stock causing problems. It resulted in a steep decline in passenger numbers.

The next company to construct a deep-level line would therefore need to ensure none of the same mistakes were repeated. It was to be known as the Central London Railway (CLR), and its investors were granted permission in 1892 to build a new line through the heart of the city that today forms much of the Central line.

The agreed route was from Bank in the City of London, where it could compete with the Inner Circle and the terminus of the C&SLR, to Shepherd's Bush. On the way it would pass through the West End and out towards the west of London, thus becoming the first underground railway to serve the city's major shopping and entertainment districts, and also some of its wealthiest suburbs.

Construction started in August 1896 with the sinking of a shaft at the site of what would become Chancery Lane station. Additional shafts were sunk along the route in the months that followed, and almost all tunnelling work had been completed two years later in 1898. The building phase had in fact run over schedule at various stages, but for the most part the new railway had been constructed with little incident.

This was due in no small part to the calibre of a familiar group of engineers and contractors whose job it was to build it. The great John Fowler, by now in his early eighties, was drafted in to oversee the project. His experience of building the Metropolitan Railway and Metropolitan District Railway was invaluable to the owners of the Central London Railway, as was that of Fowler's colleague Benjamin Baker. The two men had worked together on many railway projects across the United Kingdom, including the Forth Bridge in Scotland.

The other major figure employed to assist construction of the new railway was the omnipresent James Henry Greathead. As the man responsible for designing the tunnelling shields that were to be used, his involvement was an obvious choice, but it was also his detailed knowledge of how to construct tunnels through the London clay that was so desirable to those keen on building something bigger and better than the City & South London Railway. All three men had had some involvement with the C&SLR, and thus it was hoped that their combined experience would not only replicate the great engineering feats achieved by the previous railway, but also improve upon them.

The contractors hired to build the railway included a firm owned by John Price and another owned by Walter Scott. They would later go on to build the railway that forms much of the modern day Piccadilly line, and later Price would even develop his own version of the Greathead Shield.

The construction process was governed by a precise planning technique that draws comparison with that of the Metropolitan Railway, as much of the new route followed the path of a busy road above. This was more than just a practical decision, however.

The roads through the heart of central London and out to the west were home to some of the most lucrative horse-drawn cab routes in the city. Not only would the CLR be constructing a railway along a popular route, they would be providing its often wealthy passengers with a faster and hassle-free way to travel it.

The practical considerations of building a railway below a road were still important of course, and the CLR was able to benefit from the same freedom to build below roads that had been exploited by previous companies several years before.

Central London Railway workers inside a Greathead Shield. (©TfL from the London Transport Museum collection)

Anyone riding the Central line today would find it impossible not to notice the many sharp curves and bends during the section of the line between St Paul's and Liverpool Street, including the platforms at Bank, which are on a complete curve. The reason for this is again related to the original route following the path of a road above ground.

It allowed the CLR to take further advantage of the free access to build the railway below an established road, and also made it easier to avoid damaging some of the oldest buildings in London. The engineers and navvies who built the Metropolitan District Railway may have had to ensure they caused no damage to the Houses of Parliament when building the Inner Circle, but they were in fact a relatively new set of buildings at the time.

The builders of the CLR were contending with buildings that had a far longer history, most notably Christopher Wren's St Paul's Cathedral, completed in 1697. It was therefore more important than ever that the route should stick to following the path of the road above.

Some parts of the road were very narrow, however, which posed a new challenge for the engineers. The solution was to build such parts of the railway so that the running tunnels were constructed one on top of the other, as opposed to side by side. It placed even greater pressure on the workers to ensure that the job was completed to the highest possible degree of accuracy.

The railway opened in July 1901 and was a huge success. It wasn't long before there was more construction work to be done, with three modest extensions being completed within the first twenty years of the line opening. The first was a short addition further west to Wood Lane in 1908, followed by one at the easterly end in 1912 to Liverpool Street, in order to provide an interchange with the mainline station. Next came an extension even further west in the shape of a new set of platforms built at Ealing Broadway mainline station, opened in 1920.

The line was extended several more times between 1946 and 1957. The advance towards the north-east of London continued first to Stratford and later deep into Essex. It had reached Epping by 1949, and later all the way to the rural town of Ongar, the entire stretch between here and Loughton having been taken over from the Great Eastern Railway (GER). At the western end of the line, the route was extended in 1948 on a new branch that terminated at West Ruislip.

The various extensions had taken longer to complete than expected due to a delay in construction caused by the start of the Second World War, but the Central London Railway was able to play its own part in helping with the war effort.

When electronics firm Plessey needed a makeshift solution to the problem of their existing factory having been bombed, they gained permission to use a section of the partially built easterly extension as their new base.

The company commandeered the running tunnels between Leytonstone and Gants Hill, included both unfinished stations and the ones in between at Wanstead and Redbridge. Construction workers were able to repurpose the tunnels into a subterranean factory that was responsible for making a range of electrical equipment used in battle. Opened in 1942, the facility was large enough to accommodate thousands of workers, mostly women (see later chapter), and was even equipped with a narrow gauge railway.

The temporary factory was dismantled after the war ended, and the section of railway was finally able to open in 1947 as part of what today is the Central line's Hainault Loop. There was much new construction work required across the London Underground network after the war was over. Several stations had suffered significant bomb damage, including the CLR's own station at Bank: the result of a direct hit on the ticket hall in 1941 during the Blitz. A total of fifty-seven people lost their lives, and the station took several weeks to repair and rebuild.

The CLR had originally offered its passengers a flat rate of 2d on all tickets. The press therefore nicknamed it the 'Twopenny Tube', which quickly caught on. The financial part of the name fell out of favour when ticket prices were later increased, but the term 'Tube' was by now a part of London's vocabulary, and it was soon embraced as the casual name for the entire network. The official name change from Central London Railway to the Central line was finalised in 1937.

The involvement of John Fowler, Benjamin Baker and James Henry Greathead in the success of the Central London Railway was a fitting tribute to the distinguished careers of all three. It would also prove to be the start of a changing of the guard in the story of London's underground railways. Fowler and Greathead had both died before the Central opened. Baker would go on to help build what today is the Bakerloo line, but he too was dead by 1907. It was a new century, and the start of a new era for subterranean railway construction.

EMBANKMENT VIA EGYPT

In addition to his work on the early lines of what later became the London Underground, Benjamin Baker was also involved in the installation of one of the city's most famous monuments. After standing for more than 2,000 years in Egypt, an ancient obelisk was given to the United Kingdom in 1877 as a gift. Baker was responsible for designing the container inside which the artefact was safely shipped to London. It was renamed Cleopatra's Needle and still stands today on the Victoria Embankment, above part of the original Metropolitan District Railway/Inner Circle railway route.

3

CHARLES YERKES AND THE TWENTIETH-CENTURY RAILWAY

CONSOLIDATING THE NORTHERN LINE

The continued success of the City & South London Railway and Central London Railway paved the way for further deep-level tube lines to be built at the beginning of the twentieth century.

The three new railways that followed the completion of the CLR form the basis of what we know today as London Underground's Northern, Bakerloo and Piccadilly lines. They were built as part of huge expansion plans set in motion by American Charles Tyson Yerkes, who purchased the ailing Metropolitan District Railway in 1901.

Several smaller railway companies had been granted permission to construct new underground railways in the last decade of the nineteenth century, but each had been struggling to find the capital needed for work to start. When Yerkes arrived in London, eager to build a unified network of lines across the city, he formed a consortium of investors in order to purchase not just the Metropolitan District Railway, but also many of the other companies proposing various new lines.

Yerkes' vision of an integrated London-wide tube railway would only ever be possible if it was owned, built, managed and powered by one company. Instead of building several individual lines, Yerkes' theory was that they should in fact be combined and extended, with easy interchange between each one.

American tycoon Charles Tyson Yerkes. (©TfL from the London Transport Museum collection)

By 1902 Yerkes and his investors had founded the Underground Electric Railways Company of London (UERL). It not only allowed them to proceed with building their new railways, but also placed them in direct competition with the Metropolitan Railway.

In 1893, a new company named the Charing Cross, Euston & Hampstead Railway (CCE&HR) had obtained the necessary powers to construct a deep-level line between Hampstead in north London, and Charing Cross in central London. By the turn of the century the project had been purchased by Yerkes, and construction of the tunnels started in September 1903.

The route had by now been expanded. It would run beyond Hampstead to a new terminus at Golders Green, and there was to be an additional branch to a new terminus at Archway (opened under the name Highgate).

The arrival of Yerkes saw many Americanised ideas begin to appear for the first time on the growing underground railway system. Included in the list of various new initiatives were suggestions about how the new tunnels should be constructed, and therefore early plans for how the CCE&HR was to be built resembled the urban railways of Chicago more than those of London. Yerkes even had his own team of engineers sent over from the States to advise on best practice. There was little room for negotiation when faced with the realities of the infamous London clay, however, and so the tried-and-tested methods used to build the C&SLR and CLR were largely reused again here.

There was some scope for improvements nevertheless. In addition to the proven Greathead Shield method, the railway was also constructed using a new cutting device that had been developed by engineer John Price, known as the Price Rotary Excavator. He was one of the owners of the firm Price & Reeves, which had been contracted by Yerkes' company to manage the construction process. As noted earlier, Price was also one of the contractors who had been employed to build certain sections of the Central London Railway in the late nineteenth century.

The new device worked in a similar way to the Greathead Shield, but with motorised power used to drive several rotating arms, each equipped with a cutting blade and attached to a central shaft. It allowed for distances of up to 160ft to be tunnelled every week, and by 1905 the work was mostly complete. The rest of the work was finished by hand, thanks as ever to the dedication of hundreds of men.

As with each of the lines that had been built in the decades prior to the CCE&HR, there were many engineering challenges to overcome, plus new ones that had not been encountered before. The addition of the branch line to Archway called for a junction to be built along part of the route, close to what would become Camden Town station on opening. Junctions had been commonplace in open cutting sections of the Metropolitan Railway and Inner Circle, but this would mark the first time that such a junction had been built on any of the new tube railways, located deep below ground.

The new railway also proved to be the deepest of the deep-level lines, and still is today. At their lowest point, between Hampstead and Golders Green, the tunnels are more than 67 metres below ground. Hampstead is the deepest station on the entire network – a distinction that would have been given to a station named North End (also often referred to by its nickname, Bull & Bush). It was included in the original CCE&HR plan, but was scrapped before completion after it was calculated that few passengers would likely use it.

Further complications arose during construction of the new station at Charing Cross. It was built below the mainline railway station and therefore required some complex structural work to avoid damaging the existing buildings and platforms above.

Ironically, it was a problem that was overcome using a technique very similar to the old cut-and-cover construction methods of the previous century. A section of the mainline station forecourt was dug up so that the new platforms and lift shafts could be completed. This was then roofed over, with the forecourt rebuilt on top.

New tunnels being built on the Northern line near Camden Town. (©TfL from the London Transport Museum collection)

The CCE&HR opened for passenger use in June 1907. It was expanded over the years that followed, eventually running beyond Golders Green to Edgware, and from Archway to High Barnet. A short spur line to Mill Hill East was all that was completed of an additional extension that was scrapped after the Second World War.

The UERL purchased the C&SLR in 1913 and set about the task of combining it with the CCE&HR to form one line. The C&SLR was also extended several times, from Stockwell to Clapham Common and later Morden, and from Borough to Euston via the City of London. By 1937 both railways had been connected and the combined route was renamed the Northern line.

Construction work in 1926 at Tooting Broadway. (©TfL from the London Transport Museum collection)

Dollis Brook Viaduct on the Northern line. (Author)

KENNINGTON VIA KENNINGTON

The Northern line splits into two different branches between Camden Town and Kennington; known as the Bank branch and the Charing Cross branch. Kennington station includes an extra section of tunnel known as the Kennington Loop. It's used as a way of allowing Charing Cross branch services terminating at the station to turn around and head back in the direction they came from. Trains enter the loop after leaving the southbound platform and emerge minutes later on the northbound platform.

CROSSING THE NORTH-SOUTH DIVIDE: THE BAKERLOO TAKES SHAPE

The birth of the Northern line has a similar story to the development of what would become the Bakerloo line. It was a railway founded on the principle that a new deep-level tube line was required in order to better serve the mainline railway termini at Waterloo, providing a new connection to central London and further north.

Waterloo's awkward placement outside of the Inner Circle left it isolated from the underground lines. The Waterloo & City line had helped form a connection to the City of London, but a more substantial route was now needed.

Various proposals were put forward, and in 1893 a company known as the Baker Street & Waterloo Railway (BS&WR) successfully gained approval to build a new line between the two stations included in its name. The plan also included an extension further north to Marylebone, in order to serve the mainline railway station that would be opening in 1899.

Initial construction work began in August 1898, with the Greathead Shield method being used yet again. The work was this time undertaken by two different firms that both had connections to some of the most respected engineers of the era. The first was Perry & Company, which was responsible for most of the tunnelling work along the new route. Based in

Bow, the company's chairman was Herbert Henry Bartlett – an acclaimed designer who also worked on a long list of buildings as varied as Tower Bridge, St Thomas' Hospital and Waterloo station itself.

The other company had been founded by – and named after – John Mowlem. Originally a stonemason from Dorset, the prestigious London buildings that Mowlem had previously worked on included Somerset House and the tomb of Horatio Nelson inside St Paul's Cathedral. He died three decades before work on the BS&WR began, but his family ensured that his company lived on long after his death. The Mowlem company is still hugely successful today. They were responsible for many of the city's most famous structures in the twentieth century, including Liverpool Street station, Battersea Power Station, the House of Commons, Tower 42, the Admiralty Arch and London City Airport.

Overseeing the entire engineering project was the appropriately named Benjamin Baker. He had previously consulted on the City & South London Railway and Central London Railway projects, alongside John Fowler and James Henry Greathead.

Such esteemed company boded well for the construction process, and tunnelling commenced after two shafts had been sunk close to the north bank of the Thames. From here, work started in the direction of Baker Street in early 1899, followed a few months later by advancement in the opposite direction towards Waterloo.

This section of the new route demanded tunnelling under the river itself, and therefore the hundreds of men employed to build the tunnels would be working in compressed air. It would be a return to the same dangerous and unforgiving working conditions experienced by those who had helped construct the Waterloo & City Railway some fifty years earlier.

In an unforeseen complication, the journey below the Thames was hampered by disturbances in the earth caused by work on an aborted railway in the 1860s. Known as the Waterloo & Whitehall Railway, it had been planned as a pneumatic railway connecting Great Scotland Yard with the station at Waterloo. The project ran into financial difficulties and was never completed, but the initial dredging work had caused sufficient damage. With the BS&WR now aiming to follow almost the exact same route, the engineers were instead forced to change plan slightly, in order to avoid the damage from the previous century.

Engineer Benjamin Baker. (©TfL from the London Transport Museum collection)

As is often the case, history began to repeat itself in 1901, as spiralling costs forced work on the new railway to stop. By this point the route was now set to run further south to Elephant & Castle, for interchange with the mainline station. It would also be extended north to Paddington, to form a connection not only to the major railway termini, but also to the Metropolitan Railway and Metropolitan District Railway.

It was left to Charles Yerkes to save the day. He purchased the incomplete railway in 1902 and made it part of his growing empire. Work restarted soon after, and the line opened for passenger use in March 1906 from Baker Street to Kennington Road (later renamed Lambeth North). The section between here and Elephant & Castle was completed a few months later. The full name of the railway proved unpopular with both the press and passengers, and it was instead dubbed the Bakerloo line just a few months after opening.

It's interesting to note that although Yerkes' intervention had undoubtedly rescued the new railway, it also added to the scale of work required. In order to allow the line to fit more consistently with the other railways recently purchased by the UERL, some of the tunnel and station work had to be adapted, in particular at Oxford Circus.

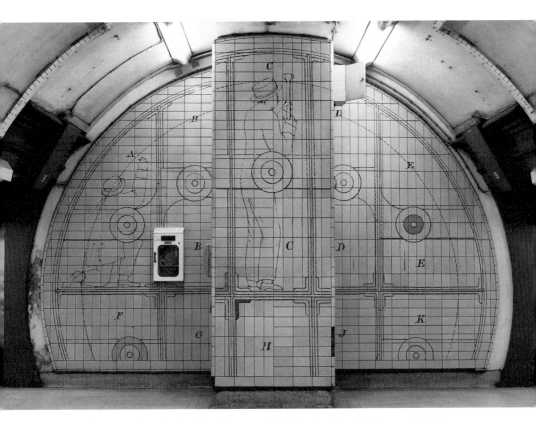

Tunnel construction depicted in tiling near the Bakerloo line platforms at Paddington station. (Author)

The push towards Marylebone and Paddington, via another new addition at Edgware Road, was complete by 1913. Two years later the line was extended further to Queen's Park, where it emerged from more than 6 miles of deep-level tunnel. From here, Bakerloo trains ran to Watford Junction on track shared with the London and North Western Railway (LNWR). Services were later scaled back, and since the mid-1980s Harrow & Wealdstone has acted as the northerly terminus.

In the 1930s a new set of deep-level tunnels was constructed between Baker Street and Finchley Road that followed a similar path to the Metropolitan Railway extension built in the previous century (see earlier). The new tunnels formed a separate branch of the Bakerloo that opened in 1939, replacing the Metropolitan services between Baker Street and Stanmore. The branch was later taken over by the newly opened Jubilee line in 1979.

MYTHS AND LEGEND

There are many conspiracy theories and urban myths about secret deep-level tunnels branching off from the London Underground. One of the most outlandish is the suggestion that Buckingham Palace has its own secret platform, allegedly reached by a spur line close to the disused station at Down Street. Another popular myth is that there is a platform below the BBC's Broadcasting House that branches off from the Bakerloo line. The line does run almost directly below the building, but it's likely that the idea of a secret platform is a corruption of stories about a Second World War bunker that was part of the original building.

THE EXTENSION THAT NEVER WAS

The huge costs and manpower required to build an underground railway mean there is very little margin for error. To avoid wasted work and resources, any proposed route or station must be planned well in advance of construction work starting. If a proposal is to be scrapped, then it's vital for the decision to be made as swiftly as possible.

Occasionally however, work has sometimes already begun when a plan changes. In the case of North End station for instance – part of the original CCE&HR route discussed earlier – some work had been completed at platform level when it was decided that the station would no longer be needed. Northern line trains today still pass through a wider section of tunnel that marks where the platforms would have been, and at street level there is a basic structure that now serves as an emergency exit and ventilation shaft.

It was a similar story elsewhere on the Northern in the 1930s, when the line was set to be extended beyond Edgware. Known as the Northern Heights project, it was scrapped after the Second World War, but only after much work had already been completed on adapting existing mainline stations and new tunnel work.

On the Bakerloo line, initial tunnelling work commenced on an ill-fated proposed extension towards south-east London. The plan had been granted approval in 1931, and would have seen the line extended from the terminus at Elephant & Castle to Camberwell, and potentially further at a later date to Herne Hill.

The project floundered for many years, but by 1950 work was ready to begin. The proposed extension was set to follow a route through much waterlogged earth, which would mean more hours working in compressed air for the men tasked with building the new tunnels.

Land was cleared in preparation for a number of shafts to be dug, and some basic work was started close to Camberwell Green. The existing tunnels at Elephant & Castle were also adapted in order to accommodate the new extension.

By late 1950, escalating costs made the project seem no longer viable and work ground to a halt. The extension was shelved indefinitely soon after and remains unfulfilled to this day. No visible traces of the initial work at Camberwell exist today. At Elephant & Castle, the tunnel enhancements are now used as sidings, where Bakerloo line trains are often stabled overnight.

FURTHER CONSOLIDATION AND THE BIRTH OF THE PICCADILLY

London's next deep-level railway formed most of what we know today as the Piccadilly line. It was to be the last project overseen by Charles Yerkes before his death in 1905, and perhaps the one that most typified his skill in combining smaller railways in order to create a bigger and better entity. In this instance, the line that opened was a combination of two separately proposed railways and an extension to an established one.

In 1897, a company known as the Brompton & Piccadilly Circus Railway (B&PCR) successfully gained approval to construct a deep-level route from Piccadilly Circus to South Kensington. The proposed railway was then purchased by the Metropolitan District Railway, which was also looking to build a new section of track from Earl's Court to Mansion House, via South Kensington.

Two years later, in 1899, another railway company had been granted permission to build what they proposed to call the Great Northern & Strand Railway (GN&SR). It was to be a route that would run from Wood Green in north London, to a terminus close to the Strand, in the heart of the theatre district.

When Yerkes' company took ownership of the Metropolitan District Railway in 1901, it brought the soon-to-be-built extension and B&PCR under his charge. Sensing the opportunity to build a line that would cut through central London from west to north, Yerkes quickly set about purchasing the GN&SR. The combined proposals were approved and renamed as the Great Northern, Piccadilly & Brompton Railway (GNP&BR).

In order for the various routes to physically become one line, a few tweaks were agreed upon. The line would still run into central London from a northerly terminus, but this would now be at Finsbury Park instead of Wood Green. It would still include a station on the Strand, which was later renamed Aldwych.

The two original routes would connect at Holborn, with new stations added between here and Piccadilly Circus at Leicester Square and Covent Garden. The station at Aldwych was downgraded to being on a short spur, operated by a shuttle service that catered primarily for theatregoers. Aldwych would close years later in 1994, but is still preserved today as a location for filming, and is occasionally opened for public tours run by the London Transport Museum.

With the complexities of the route now decided upon, building work could finally begin. The individual companies originally planning to build the lines had struggled to find the requisite funds to start construction, but with Yerkes' backing it would be a relatively quick process.

Work started in 1902 with shafts being sunk at Finsbury Park, Knightsbridge and South Kensington. As ever, the Greathead Shield method was called into action in order for tunnelling to begin from each of the three shafts. The success of John Price's advanced cutting device in speeding up construction on the Northern line saw the newer device also deployed here.

The extent of the building work that was required made it necessary for three different contractors to be employed, each assigning their own team of trusted men to head below ground for months of tunnelling work.

Workers tunnelling as part of an extension to the Piccadilly line. (©TfL from the London Transport Museum collection)

The use of Price's cutting device made his company Price & Reeves an obvious choice. The other two companies hired to build parts of the line were named Walter Scott & Middleton, and Butt & Stennett. Walter Scott's company had previously constructed the Central London Railway, along with John Price and others.

Most of the tunnelling work was complete by 1906, and the line opened for public use in December of the same year, from Finsbury Park to Hammersmith. The short branch line between Holborn and Aldwych opened the following year.

When the first cut-and-cover lines were built in the 1860s, London's roads were full of horse-drawn carts and trolley buses. By the time the Piccadilly Tube was constructed, the roads were now packed with cars. There were more than 100,000 driving licences issued across the city in the 1920s, and so several major new roads were built in order to meet the demand of what would soon become a national obsession.

Similar to how the Inner Circle was constructed as an orbital railway around central London in order to connect the mainline railway termini, construction started in the 1920s on the North Circular and South Circular roads to connect the suburbs and provide easy access into and through the centre of town.

Arnos Park Viaduct, built when the Piccadilly line was extended to Cockfosters. (Author)

With the continued expansion of the underground railways out towards the suburbs, major roads began to create a new obstacle that would need to be manoeuvred. The Piccadilly line was extended from Finsbury Park to Cockfosters in the 1930s, on a route that required the railway to cross the North Circular near to what on the opening of the line would become Arnos Grove station.

To build a bridge over a functioning road was uncharted territory for the engineers and builders working on the line, and an additional road crossing was required further north, adjacent to Arnos Grove. This time the railway was built to run beneath the road, with Bowes Road reconstructed on a section of bridge above.

Further north of Arnos Grove, between here and Southgate station, the extension onwards to Cockfosters also necessitated the construction of a viaduct that took the new railway across Arnos Park. It is an impressive structure with thirty-four individual arches, and is said to be the last brick viaduct to be built anywhere in the UK.

The Piccadilly line was extended several more times during the twentieth century, this time to the west of London. By 1933 the railway had reached Uxbridge, taking over services previously operated as part of the Metropolitan District Railway. A new branch line was also constructed in the 1930s from Acton Town to Hounslow West, again running on lines built originally by the Metropolitan District Railway.

Hounslow West remained as a terminus station until the mid-1970s, when construction began on an extension via a new set of tunnels to Hatton Cross. It was part of a project to connect the London Underground network to Heathrow, and by 1984 the line had reached the airport, with new stations serving each of its four terminals.

Construction work continued well into the twenty-first century, with a new station opened in 2008 to serve Terminal 5. The terminal was reached by new tunnels that were built using huge Tunnel Boring Machines (TBMs) – a far cry from the Greathead Shields used to construct the first section of the line over a century earlier (see later section for more on how TBMs are used today).

The change of name from the GNP&BR to the Piccadilly line was the result of the UERL being absorbed into the unified London Underground network. It was also during this period that a number of original GNP&BR stations were closed. The original section from

Finsbury Park to Hammersmith had been somewhat overzealous with the number of stops it was estimated would be needed to best serve demand. By 1934 the stations at Down Street, Brompton Road and York Road had all closed due to low passenger use. The station at Dover Street meanwhile was replaced by Green Park.

UPS AND DOWNS

The first London Underground escalator was installed at Earl's Court in 1911. Its success led to many other stations across the system having them installed, often as a replacement for lifts. Adapting a station to fit an escalator was often a huge engineering challenge, as more space was required than for a traditional vertical lift shaft. Several stations therefore had to be remodelled or even resited. A lack of space meant that it was not possible to install escalators at some stations, which is why Covent Garden, Edgware Road (Bakerloo), Elephant & Castle and various others still rely on old-fashioned lifts today.

4

A NEW GENERATION

BY ROYAL APPOINTMENT PART I:
CONSTRUCTING THE VICTORIA LINE

By 1933 the various individual railway companies had been consolidated under the control of the London Passenger Transport Board and now operated as the London Underground, as part of the London Transport network. The organisation was responsible for the city's Tube railway and its trams and buses. It had signalled the demise of both the UERL and Metropolitan Railway, as the lines of both former companies were now part of the unified network.

Several existing lines had been extended during this period, but no work was commissioned on a new dedicated line until almost three decades later, when construction started on what would open as the Victoria line.

The success of the network and the ever-increasing size of London's population were beginning to cause severe congestion at several major stations. A new line was therefore required in order to ease the pressure, in particular on the Piccadilly line.

Similar to how the original Metropolitan Railway, Metropolitan District Railway and the subsequent Inner Circle (Circle line) had been built in order to connect several mainline railway stations, the Victoria line would do the same.

The major terminus stations at Victoria, Euston and King's Cross/ St Pancras were all included along the route, in addition to busy suburban commuter stations like Highbury & Islington and Finsbury Park. The line would also provide better interchange with other Tube lines. In fact, Pimlico is the only station on the entire line that doesn't include a connection to either the mainline railway network or the rest of the London Underground.

Initial approval for the line to be built had been granted as far back as the late 1940s, albeit under a slightly different route. But just as with every other new line that preceded it, the plan stalled for many years as finances were arranged and organisational ownership of the nation's railways shifted.

By the late 1950s the route had finally been agreed. It would run from Victoria station, close to the north bank of the Thames, to Walthamstow in

Much of the Victoria line was built using a device known as a drum digger. (©TfL from the London Transport Museum collection)

north-east London. The route was then extended before work had commenced, to run below the Thames to a new terminus at Brixton.

Construction started in September 1962, with several shafts sunk along different points of the new route. As the first new deep-level railway to be constructed in several years, it would be the first to make use of new tunnelling methods that had been developed in the years since the previous tunnels had been dug.

New technologies had advanced the concept of the tunnelling shield yet again, this time in the form of a new device known as a drum digger. It was the latest in a long line of tweaks and enhancements to the original basic principles of the Greathead Shield, adding a rugged rotating drum to the centre of the shield, which was able to work a cutting wheel at greater power and speed than ever before.

The new device allowed for distances of up to 400ft per week to be tunnelled. It would even set a new record during construction of the Victoria line, when workers were successfully able to tunnel for 470ft in a single week. Crucially, the device also allowed for the excavated spoil to be removed more easily, thus eliminating much of the hard labour required by those working inside the new tunnels. In fact, the drum digger was the closest device yet to resemble the TBMs that would be developed later (see Jubilee line section for more).

The device had been developed by Kinnear Moodie, the construction company that had been contracted to complete the Victoria line. The company had a long history of working on tunnelling projects around the world, but was acquired not long after work had commenced by a Peterborough-based firm known as Mitchell Construction. They too had experience of building tunnels, especially those related to the operation of power stations. It was this particular piece of engineering expertise that would later be put to good use on the Victoria line.

The drum digger device had allowed for greater distances to be achieved in less time, but it was also fraught with problems that delayed the entire project on several different occasions. There were also sections of the route where the device struggled to penetrate the awkward nature of the London clay, forcing more traditional methods to be deployed instead.

The new method of tunnelling was also a significant change for the men employed to work it. The senior engineers who worked at Kinnear

Men working inside a tunnelling device during construction of the Victoria line.
(©TfL from the London Transport Museum collection)

Moodie/Mitchell Construction may have been well versed in how the new device worked, but those tasked with actually using it would need training and guidance. Therefore delays occurred while the various engineers and mining staff got up to speed with this new way of working.

Finding suitable labourers to work at the tunnel face also proved to be a difficult task. The early 1960s was a boom time for many new construction projects across London. It was mainly the result of continued post-war prosperity, but a relaxation on the laws governing the height of buildings also resulted in ground being broken on several new skyscrapers and large office blocks. It led to a brief but disruptive shortfall in labourers that were needed to build the new railway.

In addition to the drum digger, there were also advancements related to how the Victoria line tunnels would be lined. Until now, all of London's deep-level tube lines had been built using cast-iron sections to secure the tunnels, which were bolted together. Interlocking iron sections were trialled on part of the new Victoria line route, which was a method that had previously been used by Mitchell Construction for tunnels at some of the power stations they built.

The principle is that the weight of the earth around the tunnel exerts enough force to allow the sections of iron to interlock and therefore hold together securely. Concrete sections were also trialled on the new line, working on the same interlocking principle as the new iron segments.

Despite the teething problems experienced with the new tunnelling method, work progressed with little disruption and by 1966 most of the tunnels were complete. Slightly more troublesome were the parts of the route where major interchanges with other Tube and railway lines were being built, and one station where the work was particularly complex was Oxford Circus.

The engineers of the Metropolitan Railway and Metropolitan District Railway had had to contend with existing gas and water mains when constructing their cut-and-cover railways in the 1860s. A century on, the engineers of the Victoria line had to contend with a whole mass of subterranean infrastructure in one of London's most built-up and modernised areas.

Adding to the complexities was the problem that Oxford Circus was already served by two other deep-level tube lines, the Central and Bakerloo. The new tunnels, platforms, escalators and passageways therefore had to be built in and around the existing ones.

The task was so huge that the existing station had to be completely remodelled. Above ground, a large bridge canopy was erected above the road surface of Oxford Circus itself. It was needed to assist with the reconstruction work, but the idea was that it would also allow the road to remain open.

Having to close one of the busiest road and pedestrian intersections – where Oxford Street and Regent Street meet – would have generated as much anger and resentment as when the Metropolitan Railway had been forced to close parts of the New Road for long periods in the previous century.

The work at Oxford Circus was hampered further by the need to delicately tunnel under the lower ground floors of several major department stores, and by having to work around the rotting foundations of a number of buildings that had once stood above ground.

The work at Euston, Victoria and other interchanges with existing lines also posed many great challenges. In order for the new line to integrate with the others, a series of junctions had to be built between running tunnels. Space restrictions also meant that the new Victoria line tunnels often had to be built directly below the tunnels of existing lines. It was a demanding feat of engineering, especially considering that the existing lines were in full operation at the time.

After several years of work the Victoria line fully opened in 1972, having been completed in stages. It has since become one of the busiest lines on the network and is often heavily congested. There is little scope for extension, although there has been some debate about whether a new terminus at Herne Hill might ease some of the pressure.

WAKING THE DEAD

London is known to have many plague pits that were dug deep below ground as mass graves, in order to stop the corpses of Great Plague victims spreading the disease. Several pits were stumbled upon during the construction of London Underground's deep-level lines, leading to some grim discoveries for workers. Aldgate station is said to have been built directly above a huge pit where hundreds of bodies were buried.

BY ROYAL APPOINTMENT PART 2:
EXTENDING THE JUBILEE

The Jubilee line officially opened in April 1979. Originally to be named the Fleet Line – later changed in honour of the Queen's Silver Jubilee – it was a railway that for the most part had come ready-made. As noted earlier, much of the route was already operated for several years as a branch of the Bakerloo, between Baker Street and Stanmore, and before that as a branch of the Metropolitan.

There was some additional construction work to be undertaken, however, as the new railway would also now run further south from Baker Street via a new 2½-mile deep-level tunnel to Charing Cross. The new tunnels were built with many of the same advanced techniques that had been used to build the Victoria line in the previous decade. In addition to the tunnel work, there were new stations built at Bond Street and Green Park, and Charing Cross station was rebuilt to enable better interchange between the new platforms and those of the Bakerloo and Northern lines.

It was to be the last new construction project on the London Underground for almost twenty years, reflecting a dark period in the network's history that was characterised by a drop in passenger usage, financial struggles and major incidents. It took the company until the millennium to turn its fortunes around, helped in part by a major new extension to the Jubilee.

Proposals to extend the railway had been in discussion since before the line had even opened. The idea was that a new extension would serve vast parts of south-east London and the Docklands – at the time on the cusp of a massive regeneration project. The lack of an Underground line in this part of London had been a point of contention since as far back as the Second World War, but took on a greater sense of urgency now that the redevelopment was about to begin.

Various different planned routes were proposed and approved in the late 1970s, including branches towards the City of London and south towards New Cross and on to Lewisham. By the early 1990s the plan had changed again, and the proposal that was finally given full approval was for an extension from the existing station at Green Park to Stratford in the east. The plan called for eleven new stations, plus the closure of the original terminus platforms at Charing Cross.

It was the first major new tunnelling construction project on the London Underground since the completion of the Victoria line. The section built in the 1970s, from Baker Street to Charing Cross, may have been built in a similar fashion to the Victoria, but construction techniques had advanced significantly in the twenty years that had passed since then.

With decades of previous underground tunnelling expertise across London to draw from, the company responsible for completing the Jubilee line extension had much inspiration. But this was also an opportunity to learn from the mistakes of the past and make use of new innovations that were proving successful further afield.

Although plagued by controversy, by 1994 the Channel Tunnel project had successfully constructed a new railway under the English Channel, from Folkestone in Kent to Coquelles, near Calais. The new tunnels had largely been constructed using cutting-edge tunnel boring machines.

In basic terms, a TBM is a larger, more powerful and fully automated development of the tunnelling shields designed by James Henry Greathead and John Price, which themselves had been based on the principle of Marc Brunel's original shield.

A TBM features a large cutting wheel that rotates and therefore cuts away at the tunnel face, boring its way through the earth with relative ease and speed. The Channel Tunnel engineers had also used a construction technique known as the New Austrian Tunnelling Method (NATM), which uses the natural strength of the ground being tunnelled through in order to assist the construction itself.

The combination of TBMs and NATM had yielded impressive results, and therefore they were an obvious choice for how the Jubilee line extension would be built. Work finally began on more than 15 miles of new tunnel in December 1993, but less than a year later the safety of the NATM came into question.

It had been used during construction of new tunnels for what today is the Heathrow Express railway line from Paddington to Heathrow Airport. A section of the new tunnel collapsed, and therefore the construction of the Jubilee line was stalled while the safety concerns were investigated. The method was later certified as being safe, and the construction process was able to begin again.

Modern tunnelling techniques being used for the Jubilee line extension. (©TfL from the London Transport Museum collection)

Aside from the obvious physical advantages of TBMs, they significantly cut the amount of manpower needed to build an underground railway. For the team of engineers, construction staff and TBM operators that worked on the Jubilee line extension, it was a far less hazardous and gloomy environment. There were still plenty of challenges to overcome nonetheless.

Tunnelling below the River Thames was nothing new, but the ambitious new extension plan called for no less than four new passages under the river. The route also included a sizeable section through parts of south-east London, between Southwark and Canada Water. Historically, the various railway companies that constructed the original parts of the London Underground had tended to avoid this area, due to the awkward quality of the clay. The Greathead Shields and the teams of men armed with hand tools would have struggled to penetrate the clay decades earlier. Now, however, the TBMs were able to bore their way through with little trouble.

Despite its sophistication, the raw power of a TBM means there is a serious risk that it will cause unwanted damage to the surrounding area. This posed a major problem for the engineers, especially as the route was set to pass right through the centre of the city.

Similar to the issues that had been faced by the Metropolitan District Railway when they constructed the Inner Circle in the nineteenth century, the new extension would pass directly below the Houses of Parliament and several other famous historical sites. It required precision engineering and delicate reinforcement work in order to create a protective layer between the new tunnel bores and the foundations of the buildings above.

The extended railway was completed by 1999 and was fully opened by December. The platforms at Charing Cross have been disused ever since, but have been kept for training purposes and as a location for filming.

As noted, TBMs are an advancement of an original concept developed by Marc Brunel. Although unintentional, it was a fitting tribute to Brunel's work that the new Jubilee line extension included an interchange with what is now the London Overground's East London line at Canada Water. Its close proximity to the Thames Tunnel provided a link between old tunnelling methods and new, both of which look likely to stand the test of time for many decades to come.

SLIDING DOORS

Several of the new stations opened for the Jubilee line extension had sliding glass doors built along the edge of their platforms. They were installed primarily as a way of reducing the amount of wind felt in stations when a train approaches the platform, but they have also doubled up as a safety device that can help prevent suicides or people falling on to the tracks.

FORM AND FUNCTION:
BUILDING A LONDON UNDERGROUND STATION

Much has been written elsewhere about the incredible and stunning architecture of many London Underground stations. The efforts of designers such as Charles Holden and Leslie Green have come to define the image of the Tube network, and their fine work can still be seen today thanks to many well-preserved stations across the Northern, Bakerloo and Piccadilly lines.

The Jubilee line extension managed to successfully continue the tradition, with a series of ultra-modern yet stylishly designed station concourses. The station at Canary Wharf, for instance, has earned much critical acclaim for its design, which was the work of renowned architect Sir Norman Foster.

But just like the tunnels that connect each of these stations together and the lift shafts that take passengers below ground to board the trains, no matter how well-designed a station may be, to build one requires months of hard work by hundreds of people.

Conditions for those employed to construct a station building were undoubtedly less dangerous and oppressive than for those who worked in the tunnels below, but the men still had to battle against tight completion dates and the demands of perfectionist designers.

As the public-facing side of the railway business, each building had to be finished to a high standard. In the formative years of the network, when companies would often construct a station in haste in order to beat their competitors, builders were frequently forced to work at speeds that today health and safety measures would never allow.

Osterley station under construction in the mid-1930s. (©TfL from the London Transport Museum collection)

The finished product of stations erected at speed would often be little more than crude, wooden buildings with basic facilities. Once a new line or branch had become established, many of the basic stations needed to be rebuilt on a larger and more permanent scale. Several stations also needed to be resited to different locations, in order to accommodate the realignment of track and junction points as the network was extended.

It all added up to lots of work for the men employed to excavate the passenger walkways and lift shafts, lay the bricks, tile the walls, cut the timber and apply the various fixtures and fittings that make a station.

The work became more complex in the early to mid-twentieth century, when stations were built to impress and to allow for greater capacity. It was during this period that more emphasis was placed upon the notion that a station could be a building of style and beauty. It's at this point that Leslie Green's station designs began to impress, and the concept later came of age in the 1920s and 1930s, thanks to the work of Charles Holden and the genius of the UERL's Frank Pick.

The very idea that so many original buildings still exist today is not just testament to the men who designed them, but also the actual workers tasked with transforming each one from blueprint to functioning build-ing. The work required to design a station was in itself a hard process, of course, and it certainly took its toll on the health of Leslie Green. He died at the age of just 33, having worked frantically for several years on designs for the Piccadilly, Bakerloo and Northern lines.

Since the completion of the Victoria and Jubilee lines, new station buildings are something of a rarity today. Existing stations are sometimes revamped and remodelled (see later section), but new additions to an established line are a curiosity. One exception in recent years has been Wood Lane station on the Hammersmith & City line. It opened in 2008 as part of the redevelopment of Shepherd's Bush for the Westfield shopping centre. It marked the return of 'Wood Lane' to the Tube map, replacing two previous, long since demolished, stations of the same name.

The original Metropolitan Railway platforms at Baker Street, looking much today as they did in 1863. (Author)

5

MODERN CHALLENGES AND FUTURE EXPANSION

THE DOCKLANDS LIGHT RAILWAY

In the mid-1980s construction began on a new railway project that formed an integral part in one of the largest redevelopment plans in London's long history. The Docklands Light Railway (DLR) may not officially be part of the London Underground network, but its operation as part of Transport for London and its inclusion on the London Underground map make it worthy of mention here.

After decades of decline and dereliction, the London Docklands Development Corporation (LDDC) was created in 1981 to spearhead various different plans to redevelop this expansive area of east London. A key factor in the future success of the regeneration plan would be a new and reliable urban transit system with the potential to connect the entire area with the rest of the city. Several different plans had surfaced in the decade before the LDDC was founded, including an early draft of the Jubilee line extension that would open almost two decades later, but costs had stalled each new proposal.

It was decided that a light-rail system was the solution, and after numerous different proposed routes, permission was granted for work to start on the first phase of the Docklands Light Railway. The authorised route ran along two lines, from Tower Gateway to Island Gardens, and Stratford

Parts of the Docklands Light Railway were constructed with elevated track. (Author)

to Island Gardens. The task of building the new railway was awarded to Mowlem, the company founded in the previous century by John Mowlem, who had been responsible for building parts of the Bakerloo line. The firm Edmund Nuttall was also later drafted in to work on various extensions that followed the initial section.

Physical construction work began in 1985, assisted somewhat by the fact that large parts of the route used various sections of disused railway viaduct. However, much of the existing infrastructure required reinforcement work and new alignments.

The real challenge for the engineers came when the new network was extended. It necessitated the first of several new tunnels that have been added in the last two decades. The first was constructed when a new branch of the line was built between Bank, in the City of London, and Beckton. A tunnel was constructed via a new portal built close to the original terminus at Tower Gateway. It consisted of two separate bores, leading to a new terminus station at Bank.

Work commenced in March 1988 with TBMs similar to the ones used for the Jubilee line. Unlike the Jubilee line – or anywhere else on the London Underground network for that matter – the tunnels were constructed to a wider than average diameter. The extra space wasn't created in order to accommodate wider trains; DLR rolling stock is in fact relatively narrow. Instead, the additional diameter allowed for the tunnel to include a walkway next to the track, for use during engineering work and emergencies.

Cost, space restrictions and the limitations of previous construction techniques mean that this added feature is rarely seen inside London's other railway tunnels. It's for this reason that today, on the rare occasions that London Underground passengers are asked to evacuate a train inside a tunnel, they have to walk along the actual tracks until an emergency exit can be reached at either a current or disused station.

The TBMs handled the bulk of the new tunnelling work, but extras such as fire exits, lift shafts and maintenance tunnels were worked on by hand. It proved once again that despite great advancements in tunnelling technology, there was often still much hard work to be done by those employed by the engineering firms.

Work on the new tunnel was complete by 1990. Since then the DLR has had two additional deep-level tunnels constructed, both running below the River Thames. The first was built as part of an extension to Lewisham, completed in 1999, with portals close to the stations at Island Gardens and Cutty Sark for Maritime Greenwich. The other was constructed during an extension to Woolwich Arsenal, which opened in 2009.

When added together with the tunnels built under the Thames for the Jubilee line, and those constructed decades before for the Victoria, Northern, Bakerloo and Waterloo & City lines, there are now an incredible eleven London Underground tunnels below the river. There have also been several road, pedestrian and service tunnels constructed underneath the water, making the Thames perhaps the most tunnelled river in the world. Each one owes a debt to Brunel's Thames Tunnel, which itself is still in use today.

TBM markings inside the Crossrail station box at Woolwich Arsenal. (Author)

Other construction challenges encountered by the engineers of the Docklands Light Railway included a need to build long sections of new elevated track. Constructed high above many of the new redevelopment projects below, each new section of elevated track had to be pre-constructed offsite, and then lifted painstakingly into place.

CROSSRAIL:
A NEW SUBTERRANEAN RAILWAY FOR LONDON

At the time of writing, there are several TBMs currently working their way below the streets of London. They are constructing new tunnels for Crossrail; a major new railway network across the city that is the most ambitious and important underground rail project since the groundbreaking Metropolitan Railway was constructed in the 1860s.

The TBMs use the latest state-of-the-art technology, more advanced even than the machines used to build the Jubilee and Docklands Light Railway tunnels. The project is using a total of eight machines to construct over 26 miles of new tunnel that will carry up to twenty-four trains per hour when the new railway is completed in 2018. It will form part of the Transport for London network, connecting with the world's oldest underground railway at various different interchange stations through the heart of the city.

PARTY DOWN BELOW

The achievement of completing a deep-level tunnel is often cause for celebration. It can be especially satisfying when two TBMs meet perfectly in the middle, and workers on the Jubilee line extension often celebrated such occasions. On completion of a section of the Victoria line between Victoria and Walthamstow Central in the late 1960s, the final iron bolt fixed to the lining was painted gold to mark the occasion. It is said to have disappeared soon after!

PART 2

MAKING THE LONDON UNDERGROUND WORK

6

KEEPING THE CITY MOVING

There are many important jobs involved in the successful running of a system as complex as the London Underground. The company employs in excess of 11,500 workers, each of them playing some part towards helping millions of people move across London every day.

Because of its rich history and cultural significance to the fabric of London, working for the company is a badge of honour for many of its workers. From executives working at London Underground's HQ at No. 55 Broadway to those on the front line of passenger service, there seems to be a genuine sense of pride attached with working for this iconic organisation.

THE HUMBLE MOTORMAN

One of the most desirable and nostalgic jobs on the entire system is that of the train driver. They can work long hours and often find themselves the target of passenger frustration, but these are the men and women who literally run the network.

Today, drivers on the London Underground are identified by the rather mundane job title of 'train operator'. Historically, however, they were commonly referred to simply as 'drivers' in the steam era, and as 'motor-men' when electrified trains were introduced.

Motorman at South Harrow station in 1943. (©TfL from the London Transport Museum collection)

It is a job steeped in railway tradition. There has long been an unwritten hierarchy amongst mainline railway crew, with each type of worker being acutely aware of where they stand in the pecking order. The driver has always been at the very top, ever since the golden age of steam.

It was no different during the first few decades of what would later become the London Underground, when steam locomotives worked the Metropolitan Railway and the Metropolitan District Railway. When steam was replaced by electric trains, the motorman was still highly regarded, and was seen as superior to the guard.

The primary task of an Underground driver is to get passengers safely from A to B. There are a number of other duties involved, however, and train operators must complete a rigorous training process before being allowed to enter service.

A typical shift for a train operator includes different duties, depending at what time of the day the shift begins. For those working an early, the driver will usually board their train at one of the many depots across the system (see later).

After taking time to check any staff notices or announcements, the driver enters their designated train and performs a series of checks. In the driver's cab, everything from brakes, front and rear lights, passenger doors and announcements all need to be tested. Traction is also checked, along with several warning lights that will activate if something is not functioning correctly. The driver also walks through the train to check that fire extinguishers are in place and that all public areas are fit for passenger use.

Once in service, in addition to ensuring that the train moves from station to station, and monitoring all signals along the route, the driver must also keep in contact with their line controller, and keep passengers up to date with any issues or delays.

The train operator also ensures that all passengers can get safely on and off the train in the designated time at each station, without causing a delay in service. This is achieved with the use of CCTV cameras inside the cab or on the platform, and by hand signalling from station staff.

The safety of passengers is paramount, and much is often made of controls with intriguing names, such as the Dead Man's Handle. It is a safety device that triggers the brakes to stop a train if the driver releases the handle. The idea is that if the train operator was suddenly overcome by an illness, they would let go of the handle and the train would be forced to stop.

Train operator passing through Great Portland Street station. (Author)

It was first introduced on the Metropolitan District Railway in 1903, and in actual fact resulted in a reduction of the number of workers needed to run a train. It was typical for early electrified trains to be operated with two motormen in the cab, despite only one being needed. It was a throwback from the days of steam, where trains were always operated by a two-man team. One would drive the train, while the other would control fire and water. If something happened to one man, the other would step in to take over. With fire and water no longer an issue, and the Dead Man's Handle in place, trains now only required one person to operate them.

The ageing rolling stock on several lines means that the inner workings of a train cab are in fact very basic, with a primitive set of controls. The newer stock boasts more sophisticated and high-tech controls, although the process of driving them tends to be far simpler overall.

CCTV monitors used by drivers to ensure passengers enter and exit trains safely. (Author)

Safety device known as a Dead Man's Handle. (Author)

For drivers working the late shift, it's typical to board their train when it is already in service at a designated station along the route. At the end of the shift, the train operator must first ensure that all passengers have left their train. They are then responsible for taking the train back to the depot for overnight cleaning and maintenance, or into a siding for stabling.

SIDETRACKED

Although each line has its own depot, there are also several sidings located on the London Underground system, often hidden from public view. They were used historically as terminating points for services during off-peak hours, allowing a train to complete its run without having to go to the end of the line. Today, sidings are used mainly for stabling trains overnight, or for taking a broken-down train out of service so that delays can be avoided.

DARK TUNNELS, DARK TIMES

Becoming a train driver is often a childhood ambition, and it's an enjoyable job for most of those who make it onto the rails. Working the London Underground does have some unique downsides for the driver, however.

Verbal and sometimes physical abuse from irate or drunken passengers is not uncommon. Frequent delays, red signals and signal failure can also lead to long and lonely minutes inside tunnels. For mainline railway drivers, and indeed those on the London Underground who work lines that run primarily in open air, having to delay a train perhaps doesn't always feel so bad.

But for drivers on the deep-level lines it can mean staring into a pitch-black tunnel while they sit alone inside a cramped and often decades-old cab. It's an eerie environment where the mind can sometimes play tricks, and it's therefore no surprise that some drivers have described seeing and hearing many strange things deep in the tunnels.

Drivers on the Underground also have to deal with the horrific realities of suicide and people falling on to the tracks. There are an average of around sixty to eighty such deaths a year, most being suicidal passengers jumping in front of trains.

Known amongst staff as a 'one under', it can be an all too common occurrence. London has become rather cynical towards such incidents, often pointing out the selfishness of how the actions of a single person can cause such disruption to so many. It's an understandable but callous way of looking at what is still the tragic death of someone who was clearly in despair.

In his incredible book *Londoners*, author Craig Taylor includes accounts from eyewitnesses of Tube suicides. One passenger describes seeing a woman jump in front of a train in vivid detail, and of how the impact was so severe that it was almost as if the woman disappeared into thin air. Suicides such as this can be mortifying for the family of the victim, but they are just as devastating for the driver of the train.

Immediately after a suicide, there are a series of grim practicalities. Once the relevant alarms have been raised, the driver and other station staff must inspect the victim to ascertain if they are dead or alive. The driver then often has the gruesome task of pulling the train back so that the body can be removed by the emergency services.

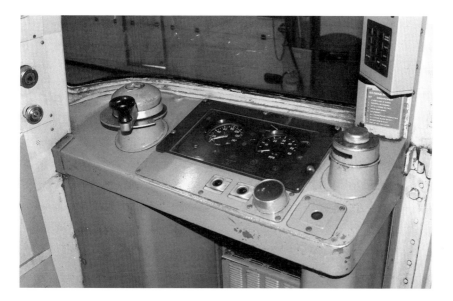

Basic controls inside the 1967 Stock, formerly used on the Victoria line. (Author)

The driver involved then has to be interviewed by the police and checked to ensure they have no traces of alcohol or drugs in their system. It is almost always clear to everyone involved that the driver was at no fault, but cases still have to be investigated so that a verdict of death by suicide can be agreed, or accidental death for those that fall on to the tracks.

Staff are trained in how to deal with incidents such as this, but nothing can fully prepare you for something this upsetting. Driver Robert Griffiths details his own experiences as a driver on the Central line in the book *Mind the Doors!* He has been unfortunate enough to have two people jump in front of his train, each one having a massive impact on his life. Griffiths describes feeling numb and in shock immediately after the incidents, and how it takes weeks to recover from such a harrowing experience.

The stress can often lead to other illnesses, and it can be a major knock to a driver's confidence. London Underground has trained counsellors on hand to speak to those affected, which can often involve returning to the station in order to face the reality of the situation and rebuild confidence. For some the experience is too much; they either leave the company altogether or request to be redeployed in a different role away from working the lines.

The change from motorman to train operator has seen the job lose some of its esteem, although in practice it is a title more in tune with the actual responsibilities of the modern driver. Since the introduction of Automatic Train Operation on the Victoria line in 1968 (see later section on the Tube Upgrade Plan), and its subsequent addition to other lines, drivers are often now required to do little more than push a basic set of buttons.

Their role is still vital in the safe and effective running of the service, but many of the special skills required by their predecessors now go unused. With all other lines due to be adapted for ATO, it seems as though the next generation of drivers will know little about the prestige of the motormen.

DEATH BY TRAIN

Suicide has been a tragic problem faced by the London Underground since the beginning. One of the earliest recorded death-by-suicide incidents occurred in 1868 when a man is said to have thrown himself in front of a train at Edgware Road. Preventing suicides is difficult, but many deep-level stations have what are commonly known as 'suicide pits' below the section of track that runs along a platform. The idea is that a person who jumps on to the tracks will fall into the trench below, and therefore not necessarily be hit by a train. It also makes it easier to remove a body that has been struck. The device is also effective in preventing harm to those who accidentally fall on to tracks. Ironically, the trenches were not designed for this reason, and were originally installed for drainage.

STATION STAFF

Other important passenger-facing jobs include the various positions filled by station staff. There are workers such as those behind the counter selling tickets and travel passes, and the customer service assistants positioned in areas such as the ticket gate and on platforms. It's their job to field any questions, assist anyone who needs help using the station and to keep all facilities clean, safe and tidy.

Important jobs in a busy Tube station include running the ticket office. (Author)

Stations also have a control room, where open communications are kept with the line controller. Announcements and service updates are made from here, and it's also where each station's CCTV cameras are monitored.

Workers on the London Underground abide by a set of rules and procedures, but the company also has a sense of humour that allows its staff to build a rapport with passengers where appropriate, and it's often amongst station staff that you can find unique characters. From boisterous and comical platform announcements to station supervisors who allow their staff to write 'thoughts of the day' in ticket halls, these are the little quirks that sometimes manage to raise a smile on the faces of busy commuters.

Kiosk used by customer service assistants. (Author)

Away from the public eye, there are those who work behind the scenes at larger control rooms at various points across the system. Every train in service can be monitored from here, and split-second decisions often need to be made to avoid major disruption. Similar to air traffic control, it can be a highly stressful job, particularly during rush hour or when London is hosting a major event.

A FAMILIAR VOICE

There is one type of worker on the London Underground that is heard by millions every day but never seen: the person who records the automated messages on trains and inside stations. Voice-over artists who can currently be heard on Central, Piccadilly, Bakerloo and District line trains include Emma Clarke and Julie Berry. The famous 'mind the gap' announcement has been voiced by several people, including television and radio actor Tim Bentinck. In 2013 the recording of this phrase at Embankment station was restored to an older version voiced by Oswald Laurence. His widow requested that London Underground reinstate it so that she could hear her beloved husband's voice again.

THE LOST WORKERS OF THE UNDERGROUND

There are some jobs on the London Underground that have disappeared as organisational changes have taken hold and as rolling stock operation has been improved. The most significant of these lost jobs is that of the guard.

Although not considered as important as the motorman, the guard was the worker who ran a train once it was in service. At the start of a shift, they would assist with the same safety checks that today are handled by the train operator alone. The guard would then ride inside one of the train carriages, in a designated section that was off limits to passengers. Here they would have their own set of controls and safety devices.

The job of the guard was primarily to ensure that all passengers got on and off trains safely, and to check that all doors were closed before leaving

Guard manning the doors at Watford station in 1964. (©TfL from the London Transport Museum collection)

the station. If the doors were closed properly, a signal known as a pilot light would illuminate, showing that it was safe to proceed. The guard would then signal to the motorman that they could now leave the station. They were also trained to drive a train during an emergency, but were only permitted to do so for short distances, such as to the next station or a designated siding or depot.

Although train operators can today be the victims of abuse from passengers, they at least get to stay inside the safety of their cab for most of their shift. Guards were in the public part of the train and were therefore vulnerable to verbal and physical violence.

As London Underground rolling stock began to become more automated, the need for a guard lessened, and the role was gradually phased out in the latter part of the twentieth century. The last ever Underground train with a guard ran in 2000.

A ticket collector at work in 1950. (©TfL from the London Transport Museum collection)

Automated ticket lines led to the demise of the ticket collector. (Author)

Becoming a guard was often used as a way of rising through the ranks on the way to becoming a motorman. After the role was disbanded, many guards successfully made the transition to driver or were moved to different roles within the company. The various controls in the guard's section of a carriage were removed, but it was still possible to see where they once were for several years after the role was withdrawn.

Another type of worker no longer seen on the Underground is the ticket collector. Before the late 1960s, access to platforms was only granted if passengers showed a ticket to a member of staff. This would either be collected or punched, and the passenger was then allowed to proceed. The opening of the Victoria line saw automated ticket lines introduced for the first time. Their success ensured that they were implemented across other lines within a few years, and it rendered the ticket collector obsolete – nothing more than a relic from the old-generation railway.

7

MAINTENANCE AND UPGRADE

The London Underground operates between the hours of approximately 5 a.m. and 1 a.m. Millions of passenger journeys are made during those twenty-one hours, across 250 miles of track and through 270 different stations. Keeping the system moving is a constant uphill battle for Transport for London, and they rely on the dedication of hundreds of staff every day.

Signal failure, defective track and escalator problems are just a few of the many issues that can regularly go wrong, and even the slightest delay in service can quickly escalate into chaos for commuters. There are technicians and contractors on-hand that can be called upon to repair such problems, whether they occur in the miles of tunnel or along an open-air section of track. It's a stressful environment for the highly skilled engineers employed as technical officers, each one under immense pressure to fix the fault and get trains moving again quickly.

The reasoning behind this type of unseen work is often hard to justify to frustrated commuters. Those waiting on a crowded platform for ten minutes would perhaps rightly question why it takes so long for a signal failure to be fixed. But in practice, the decision to suspend services due to an issue like this is one that has been made at a control room in order to keep those same passengers safe.

Above: Maintenance train at Moorgate station. (Author)

Below: Outdoor track repair work in the early 1950s. (©TfL from the London Transport Museum collection)

DOWN IN THE TUBE STATION AT MIDNIGHT

Some important maintenance and repair jobs are undertaken at weekends (see later), but other jobs cannot wait for a full weekend closure. Plus, some lines are so integral to the movement of people across the city that a series of weekend closures would be almost impossible to justify. In situations such as this, the work must be carried out at night, when time is even more pressing. With a mere four hours in which to have all work complete, it can be an extremely tense and difficult environment for the workers.

London is a very different place in the middle of the night. While most of its inhabitants are at home sound asleep, the city keeps moving. It's the time when thousands of men and women work tirelessly to fix up and clean London, removing the detritus from the previous day, in preparation for the next. The Underground is no exception.

Pass by some Tube stations in the early hours of the morning and it's sometimes possible to witness a hive of activity. Hours after the last trains of the day have left, you can often find station doors open, lights ablaze and people walking in and out.

On closer inspection these are not commuters or tourists. Instead everyone is wearing hi-vis jackets, hard hats and boots. These are the teams of workers who descend into the miles of tunnel and onto the tracks to repair and maintain everything from track to wiring, platforms to tunnel linings.

The safety of workers is the most obvious issue, and therefore the most important part of any work session is the moment when power to the electrified lines is switched off – all 400+ volts of it. After that workers are free to take to the tracks and complete their tasks, usually concentrating on a defined section of the system, with one station as a starting point and another as the end.

Engineers are not the only workers who operate across the network during the night. This is also the time when cleaners are deployed to make each station shine before the next day's passengers begin to arrive.

While the daytime cleaners work hard to remove an endless amount of free newspapers and other litter from the platforms and escalators, it's the responsibility of the night-time shift to clean floors, signage and platform furniture.

As with urgent repairs, cleaning is the kind of work that often goes unnoticed by the millions of passengers who use the London Underground every day. Take those cleaners away, however, and the same passengers would quickly notice the negative effect that not having cleaning staff would have on their journey.

Perhaps the most thankless cleaning job of all is the work undertaken by a team of workers known by the nickname 'Fluffers'. Once power to the rails has been safely turned off, the fluffers' job is to walk along the tracks, through station platforms and deep into the tunnels. It's their responsibility to clean the rails, conductor shoe gear, insulator supports and tunnel linings, in order to remove dust, grime, human hair, litter and various other pieces of undesirable material they might find. If not removed it can affect points and signals, and therefore cause delays. A build-up of dust could also create a fire hazard.

Left: A modern worker with protective clothing keeps the tunnels free from litter and debris. (©TfL from the London Transport Museum collection)

Opposite: Tunnel cleaners near Camden Town in 1930. (©TfL from the London Transport Museum collection)

The miles of running tunnels are pitch black during daytime operation, but workers such as the fluffers are assisted by lighting that is switched on in each section of tunnel being worked. It's still a dark and eerie place to work nonetheless, echoing the experience of the men who actually constructed the tunnels many years ago. Fluffing is a job that was formerly handled almost exclusively by women (see later chapter), but today there is a broad selection of workers willing to take on this dirtiest of tasks.

Advertising has been a prominent feature of London Underground stations since the very beginning. In fact, contemporary photographs of some of the oldest lines on the entire system show platform walls covered with so many adverts that it was often hard for passengers to pick out the name of a station.

Billboards and posters are slightly less intrusive in modern stations, but the walls are still covered with messaging for a huge range of products and services. Night-time is when billboards are updated, and even this is a job that requires extra skills unique to the Underground. Replacing posters along the flat walls of walkways and along the passenger side of a platform is fine, but the curved shape of the trackside wall of many platforms makes the job trickier. It's necessary for workers to place their ladder on the tracks, and work at a curved angle in order to change each section of large poster.

Many stations in central London also now have digital advertising along escalators and projected messaging on platform walls. The operating systems and software for these are also checked during the night.

A worker updates a billboard at St John's Wood station in 1957. (©TfL from the London Transport Museum collection)

BEWARE THE RAT RACE

In addition to having to contend with thick dust and debris found inside Tube tunnels, fluffers and other track workers can sometimes be at risk from the threat of Weil's disease (officially known as Leptospirosis). It can spread to humans when they come into contact with water that has been infected by rats or mice, both of which are common inside the deep-level tunnels.

LINE DEPOTS

Each of the eleven lines on the London Underground has its own depot, where trains are stabled during the night. Some lines have their depot at one of their terminus stations. Others have them located part way along their route, where space permits, while others have theirs in an area that doesn't actually form part of their line route. In instances such as this, the depots are accessed via special tunnels or spur lines that take trains away from the main passenger route.

Depots for each line are located in the following places. Bakerloo line: Stonebridge Park, London Road, Queen's Park. Central line: Ruislip, Hainault, White City. Circle and Hammersmith & City lines: Hammersmith. District line: Hammersmith, Upminster, Ealing Common. Jubilee and Metropolitan lines: Neasden, with an additional depot for the Jubilee at Stratford Market. Northern line: Golders Green, Morden. Piccadilly line: Cockfosters, Northfields. Victoria line: Northumberland Park. Waterloo & City line: Waterloo.

The depot is where a shift for a train operator usually starts or ends, in particular on those lines where the depot is located at one end of the route. It's from here that operators on the morning shift will take the driver's seat and manoeuvre their train into service. For the train operator on a late shift, part of their duties includes driving their train back to the depot for overnight stabling, with each train being designated a specific road.

Once a train has been stabled for the night, it's time for yet another team of cleaning staff to step on board and ensure that the train is sanitised and ready for the next day. It's a tough and often long process that involves cleaning the floors, windows, handrails and seats in each carriage. Trains can quickly become covered in litter, especially free newspapers and coffee cups. Cleaning staff at stations ensure that this is kept under control during the day, but the overnight teams at each depot are granted enough time to give trains a more thorough cleansing. Considering this is a job that is done after the last set of passengers of the night, the cleaners often have to contend with takeaway food debris, vomit, urine and various other delights left by thousands of late-night revellers.

Left: The Bakerloo line depot at London Road. (Author)

Opposite: Depot worker cleaning the exterior of a train in the 1950s. (©TfL from the London Transport Museum collection)

Depots are also where trains are maintained, tested and repaired. Mechanics check trains on a nightly basis to ensure they are in safe working order. In addition, every train in service is given a more rigorous health check roughly every three weeks. This involves a larger team of mechanics testing everything from the motor, wheels and brakes of each car, to passenger alarms and automated announcements.

The long and eventful life of a London Underground train means they can often become damaged, either through wear and tear, or as a result of minor collisions with debris on the tracks or acts of vandalism. Repairs to fix affected trains are carried out in several of the depots, with skilled engineers that specialise in each different type of rolling stock. As with almost every other category of maintenance job on the system, repair work is often a race against time, as a delay in getting a train back into use can have a negative impact on service levels.

Mechanic working on a District line train at a depot in 1952. (©TfL from the London Transport Museum collection)

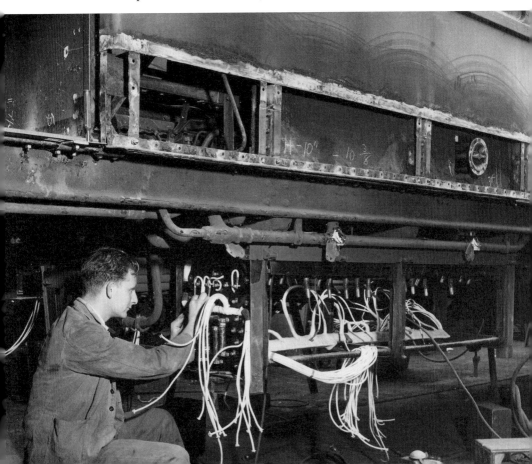

THE DRAIN BY CRANE

The Waterloo & City line is completely below ground and isolated from the rest of the network. Elsewhere on the system, junctions allow trains from one line to cross over to another if need be, such as when rolling stock needs to be taken out of service. This is not possible on the Waterloo & City line, and therefore whenever a train needs to be taken off the line for major repair work, a crane is used to haul it to street level, via a portal located near to Waterloo mainline station. It's a complex and expensive procedure, but fortunately most repairs can be undertaken at the line's own depot.

UPDATING A VICTORIAN RAILWAY

The world's oldest underground railway is one of London's proudest assets, but it's also one of its biggest downfalls. The age of the network is a serious and pressing issue. Parts of the network's infrastructure have changed little in more than a century, and there are many stations in desperate need of repair.

Therefore, in addition to the various forms of daily maintenance and running repairs, TFL have also been working on a complete upgrade to the entire system. Officially known as the Tube Upgrade Plan, it was started in 2006. The bulk of the work is due to be complete by 2016, with additional elements set to be finished between 2018 and 2021. It's a massive undertaking that involves hundreds of different workers across each of the eleven lines. It's something of a never-ending task, as by the time the upgrade work is complete, it will likely be time to start some of the work again. For now, though, billions of pounds are being spent on a range of different improvements.

A huge part of the current upgrade plan involves long periods of engineering work that is needed to replace ageing parts of the system. Taking into consideration the fact that the London Underground runs seven days a week, with just a few hours of downtime during the night, the only viable option in order for vital work to be completed is to close parts of the network during the weekend.

Platform roundel at Great Portland Street, in need of some attention. (Author)

It has been the bane of weekend travellers for several years, with thousands of people having to rely on replacement buses or alternative routes during closures. It's not uncommon for a line such as the Circle, one of the oldest on the entire system, to be closed for the duration of a whole weekend. Large sections of the Metropolitan are also regularly closed, along with various other parts of the system.

As painful as closures can be for passengers, they are a necessary means to an end, and the hope is that in the long term those same passengers will benefit from an improved service once the upgrades are complete.

A broad selection of projects are included in the upgrade plan, ranging from basic paintwork and ceiling repair, to full-scale station refurbishments. Some of the busiest and most heavily congested stations on the system, such as Bank and Victoria, are in the process of having their escalators and passenger walkways adapted, in order to create better passenger flow. The stations at Tottenham Court Road, Farringdon, Bond Street and Paddington, meanwhile, are undergoing massive change in preparation for interchange with Crossrail.

The hundreds of engineers, builders, electricians and other labourers that are working on the upgrade tend to be hidden away behind the scenes, in order to cause minimal disruption while each station remains in service.

Even less visible to the public eye are the workers helping to improve the network by making changes at track level and inside the tunnels. One of the biggest projects in the upgrade plan is a new signalling system being installed on the Northern line. As on the mainline railways, signal boxes were once commonplace on the London Underground, with most early stations having one at the end of their platforms. Signalling was gradually automated in the late 1970s and the 1980s, and the improvements on the Northern line aim to use the latest technology to increase passenger safety and cut journey times. It's interesting to note that a small selection of stations still have their signal box intact. You can see disused examples at Liverpool Street, Barbican, Chorleywood, Boston Manor and more.

There are other enhancements that will also go largely unnoticed, particularly those related to the operation of various control rooms across each line. As the nerve centres of the system, such places are where every train is tracked, and therefore improvements to monitoring systems can help staff keep trains flowing more efficiently, respond to delays quicker, and make better use of CCTV in order to allow passengers to feel safer.

PROGRESS ROLLS ON

One type of London Underground worker upon which the upgrade is having a major impact is the train operator. In addition to much of the system's station, tunnel and track infrastructure being decades old, so is most of its rolling stock. It's not uncommon for trains to work for upwards of fifty years, carrying millions of passengers during their life in service.

For instance, the 1972 Stock in operation on the Bakerloo line has been in use since the year it is named after. Similarly, the Piccadilly line stock has also been in use for well over forty years. Even on those lines where the trains seem newer, such as the Jubilee (1996 Stock) and Central (1992 Stock), the trains are still more than fifteen years old.

The upgrade plan has seen much of the oldest stock on the system replaced by a new generation of trains. It has been a huge change for the drivers who work them every day. The first line to have its stock updated was the Victoria. From 2009–11, the 1967 Stock was gradually phased out and replaced by 2009 Stock. Train operators have therefore had to re-train in order to become familiar with the new trains and change the way they have worked for years, often decades.

On the Metropolitan line, the 51-year-old A Stock trains were phased out between 2010 and 2012. Drivers were again forced to re-train, but the removal of this stock in particular has been more painful for staff.

It would be a stretch for even the most dedicated enthusiast to disagree that the A Stock trains were dated, big and cumbersome, but they were also loved by many. The trains were ingrained in a sense of nostalgia for the history of the London Underground that never fails to capture the imagination of the public, and many of the train operators on the Metropolitan had been proudly driving them for years. The switch to the new S Stock has in fact been so difficult that a number of Metropolitan drivers have decided to take early retirement rather than learn how to adapt to the new trains.

Retired 1967 Victoria line Tube stock. (Author)

Inside the cab of the Metropolitan line's A Stock. (Author)

At the time of writing, S Stock trains are also being rolled out across the District, Hammersmith & City, and Circle lines. It will mean the same re-training process for the train operators working those lines. There is also a lot of nostalgia attached to parts of these routes, including the oldest section on the entire network, and it means there will likely be train operators taking early retirement here too.

DRIVERLESS TRAINS

One of the most controversial developments for both train operators and passengers is the debate over what are generally, and somewhat inaccurately, referred to as driverless trains. In recent years, the media has reported that Transport for London is planning to introduce automatically operated trains, similar to those used on the Docklands Light Railway.

It has caused much outrage among passengers, with safety the main concern. In reality, the London Underground has been using what is officially known as Automatic Train Operation (ATO) for decades. Victoria line trains have been running with ATO since the line opened in 1968, and Jubilee and Central line trains were also adapted for ATO in the late 1990s. The other lines will also later be adapted as part of the upgrade plan.

The key difference is that ATO trains still have a driver on board, inside the cab at the front of the train. Train operators still have responsibility for the opening and closing of doors, and for pressing buttons when trains are ready to leave. They can also take manual control of a train during an emergency, and therefore their presence helps to reassure passengers that their safety is being maintained.

The so-called driverless trains being considered would potentially not have a train operator on them at all, and it's this difference that has caused concern over safety. For London Underground staff and the unions, the worry is that traditional drivers would no longer be needed, which would lead to mass redundancies.

The controversy surrounding the proposals has led to TFL suggesting that there are in fact no immediate plans to introduce completely driverless trains in the foreseeable future, and that trains would always still have a member of staff on board. The fate of train operators therefore appears to be safe, at least for now.

8

WOMEN ON THE UNDERGROUND IN WARTIME LONDON

It seems almost contrived to include a chapter about the role of women on the London Underground, but their unique contribution to the history of the network and its workforce deserves special mention.

In the first decade of the twentieth century there was little choice for any woman with a desire to work for either the mainline railways or London Transport. The few that were employed by companies like the Metropolitan Railway and Underground Electric Railways Company of London Limited tended to be assigned menial roles such as cleaners, typists or canteen workers. The career prospects for women were about to improve, however, albeit as a result of a dramatic twist in world events.

The First World War began in 1914, and by the following year thousands of British men had been called up to fight in the conflict. It created a worker shortage across many different industries, most of which would need to continue running at full capacity throughout the war.

The logical solution was to fill the void by assigning jobs to women. The unions were sceptical at first, as were the owners of many of the companies that now had no other choice but to allow their operations to be run by what was cruelly considered to be an inferior gender.

By mid-1915 the underground railways had hundreds of female workers in place. No longer confined to menial roles, they were now able to assist with every aspect of how a typical station was run. Jobs assigned to the

new workforce included ticket collectors and porters, and light maintenance work needed to keep trains running.

Maida Vale was one station in particular where the role of women
would prove to be essential. The station opened in June 1915 as part of
the extension to the Bakerloo line from Paddington to Queen's Park (see
earlier chapter). It was run entirely by female staff on opening, with eight
women undertaking every single duty.

The wages earned by women workers were inevitably lower than their
male counterparts. Driver and guard positions were also still reserved
mostly for men, but overall the war had had a positive impact on the
female workforce. When the conflict ended, the men steadily returned to
their day jobs. For now the thousands of new female workers were obliged
to return to their pre-war jobs, but they would soon be called into action
again, on a far bigger scale.

It's an unfortunate concept that the advancement of women workers was
so dependent on deadly wars, but there is no denying that the very notion of
female staff on the Tube network came of age during the Second World War.

The gap in the workforce left by men called into battle was far greater
than during the first war, and therefore more women than ever were
drafted in. This time, the long and sustained nature of the battle made it
clear that women would no longer be required merely for general station
duties. Thousands were trained to work as guards and signalmen, allowing
them to work on running trains for the first time.

Women were also handed the opportunity to work in maintenance and
engineering roles. They were given training on how to service and repair
signals and cables, and in the heavy mechanics involved with keeping rolling stock in operation. The only significant job role that stayed male-only
was that of train driver.

Elsewhere, and away from actual stations and depots, more women
were needed to fill a greater demand for the more trivial but no less vital
jobs that had already been undertaken by women for many years, such
as cleaning, catering and administrative roles at London Underground's
headquarters at No. 55 Broadway.

The disruption and general anxiety across wartime Britain highlighted a
greater need for clear and reassuring publicity and signage. It was another
area in which women were able to contribute, working in the company's
design and communications departments.

Female guard working on the Metropolitan Railway in 1917. (©TfL from the Londong Transport Museum collection)

CARING FOR LONDON'S SHELTERERS

One of the most vital contributions made by women in the war years came during the Blitz, which devastated the streets of London from 1940–41. When the first airstrikes struck, thousands of frightened Londoners looked for somewhere safe to take refuge. Naturally, they turned to the many Underground stations for shelter.

London Underground was at first against the idea of allowing people to use their various platforms and running tunnels. The fear was that the shelterers would interrupt the running of the system and create safety risks, and also that once people were down there, they would be reluctant to leave.

To a certain extent their predictions were correct, but pressure from desperate Londoners gave them little choice. People were soon allowed to use stations, including some that had become disused. They were brought back to life for this most bizarre but life-saving public service. Shelterers were also allowed to use stations still in operation, however, and therefore each one had to be run with order and rules, so that they could continue to function during operating hours.

Women delivered supplies to those Londoners using Underground stations for shelter during the Second World War. (©TfL from the London Transport Museum collection)

The people of London who were using Tube stations for shelter were undoubtedly grateful, but morale and supplies would often be painfully low. It was left to the female workforce to ensure that conditions were as comfortable as possible.

Teams of women were deployed to source, arrange and distribute food and drink to the many women and children spending night after night in the stations. They also did the same with books and toys, allowing the panicked families to take their mind off the horrors that were being suffered above ground.

Women were also tasked with helping to make conditions in the platforms and tunnels more habitable, and there were even contests run to see which station could be made the most comfortable for its shelterers.

Perhaps the most commendable aspect of this incredible contribution was that these women were volunteering their time without expecting to be paid. Their effort and hard work helped to make an awful situation more bearable for thousands of Londoners during long and terrifying nights.

As seen earlier, a section of unfinished extension to the railway between Leytonstone and Gants Hill was repurposed during the Second World War as a makeshift components factory for use by Plessey. Out of the more than 4,000 people that were said to have worked in the temporary facility, over 2,000 were women. Duties included working on a factory production line to manufacture wiring for bombers and telecommunication equipment for use in the field. Women worked in two shifts for a period of four years, day and night, and also operated the narrow gauge railway that was installed as part of the facility.

Women also assisted with the massive clean-up operation that was required after several London Underground stations were damaged or destroyed by direct hits. Stations across almost every part of the network were affected, often resulting in loss of life for shelterers and station staff alike. Some of those stations worst hit included Whitechapel, St Mary's (now disused and mostly demolished), Balham, Moorgate, Paddington and Bank.

The reconstruction process generated much new work for the hundreds of men who had built them in the first place. In some instances, stations had only been open a short time before they were bombed. Thanks as ever to the dedication of many men and women, each damaged station was brought back into operation as quickly as possible.

Women workers inside the makeshift wartime factory operated by Plessey. (©TfL from the London Transport Museum collection)

Another positive outcome gained from the rise of women workers on the London Underground during the Second World War was the social impact. Their contribution empowered many to want to continue to work after the war had ended, and do more than simply stay at home. Crucially, unlike after the First World War, many workers on the network were able to keep their jobs instead of having to hand them back to men.

Working on the Underground during the war also gave housewives and mothers the chance to interact and socialise with other women.

THE FLUFFIES

There is one particular job that was undertaken by women on the London Underground that deserves an extra-special mention. As explored earlier, the role of the fluffer is today undertaken by anyone brave and dedicated enough to stomach cleaning the miles of tunnel across the system. But in the 1940s it was a job reserved almost entirely for women, more than likely based on the assumption that cleaning was 'women's work'.

Tunnels being cleaned by the fluffies. (©TfL from the London Transport Museum collection)

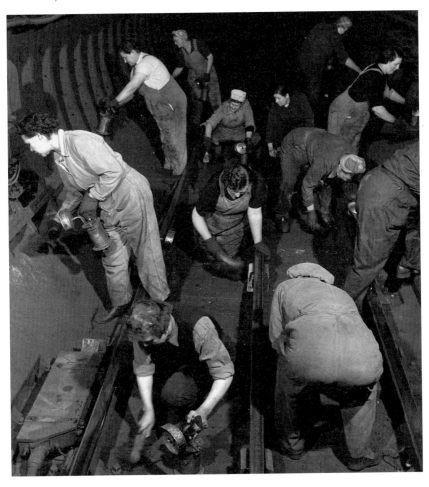

First woman Tube driver Hannah Dadds. (©TfL from the London Transport Museum collection)

A British Pathé newsreel filmed in 1944 shows a team of female workers entering the tunnels after the last train in order to clean them. Nicknamed the 'Fluffies', the women are shown working all through the night, on hands and knees dusting the rails, conductor shoes and tunnel linings in order to remove dust and other debris that could otherwise have caused a fire.

The film footage seems to suggest that the women enjoyed the sense of camaraderie between them, but in reality this must have been a difficult and depressing job. It's interesting to note that the foreman on the team is, predictably, a man. The presumption is that in the 1940s, women were free to fill many of the undesirable roles, and those that had come in such good use during the war, but were not yet suitable for any sort of managerial or supervisor position.

THE FIRST WOMAN TUBE DRIVER

The two world wars had allowed women workers to become a permanent feature on the London Underground, but there were still no women train drivers on the network even in the late 1970s. It would be unfair to suggest that this was solely the result of bullying or an unwelcoming attitude to the concept of a woman driving a train from the male-dominated railway fraternity. This was indeed a problem, but the lack of women was also down to the fact that such jobs were seldom promoted as being an attractive proposition for them.

What was needed was a pioneer, and it came in the shape of an ordinary woman in her late 20s, born in Forest Gate, east London. Hannah Dadds had become bored of her job by 1969 and decided to apply for a position with London Underground as general station staff. She was given a job as a ticket collector, and spent most of the 1970s working in a range of different roles, including working on the trains as a guard.

Hannah then applied to become a driver, which was the natural career progression. The training programme would prove to be extra tough. She would often find herself being asked more questions than anyone else in the class, likely the result of an overly sceptical trainer. There was also bullying and negative comments from other drivers to contend with.

It was not enough to deter Hannah, though, and she officially became the first woman Tube driver in October 1978, on the District line. Her sister Edna also later joined the company, and they worked together for several months as driver and guard on the same train.

Hannah took early retirement in 1993 and died in 2011 aged 70. The legacy of what she achieved still lives on today and serves as an inspiration for the next generation of women drivers. The London Underground of the twenty-first century is still male-dominated, but there is a growing number of female train operators on the network, thanks to several recruitment drives aimed directly at women.

Another inspirational figure is Hanne Bingle. During her time as a driver on the Victoria line she worked hard to promote the rights of women on the network, and was awarded an MBE in 2009.

9

DISASTER AND TRIUMPH

One of London's biggest strengths is its resilience. For every high there is often a tragic low, but for centuries the people of London have held firm in the face of everything from deadly plagues, devastating fires, floods, and two world wars.

The London Underground has had more than its fair share of dark times. During the Second World War hundreds of workers helped to keep services running, despite the loss of life when stations suffered direct hits, or horrific incidents like the crush that killed 173 people as they tried to enter Bethnal Green station looking for shelter from an air raid.

There have been other times, however, when the blame for accidents has been pointed in the direction of the company itself, and even towards individual members of staff. The most infamous examples of such cases came in the wake of a deadly train crash on the Northern line, and a horrific fire at one of the busiest stations on the entire system.

TRAGEDY AT MOORGATE

In 1975, an incident occurred at Moorgate station that today still stands as the largest loss of life on the London Underground outside of wartime or an act of terrorism. It happened on the former Great Northern & City Railway between Drayton Park and Moorgate, which, as discussed earlier, was for a period part of the Northern line, and was nicknamed the Big Tube.

An experienced motorman named Leslie Newson was working a peak rush-hour train on the morning of 28 February. At approximately 8.46 a.m., Newson's train arrived into the platform at Moorgate. But instead of slowing down, the train continued at a speed of around 35mph.

The end of the platform featured a section of overrun tunnel, plus a red warning light, sand, and a buffer stop, all of which were in place to stop a train with failing brakes. The speed and power of the six-car train were too great for the safety devices, however, and the train proceeded to crash through each barrier. The train continued to move until coming into full contact with a wall.

This being the Big Tube, the tunnels had been constructed for trains of mainline railway size. In a cruel twist of irony, the extra tunnel width gave the impacted Tube train enough room to buckle and break, adding to the damage already sustained by the head-on collision. A total of forty-three people were killed, including Newson, and more than seventy others sustained injury. The damage was significant enough to disrupt service for several days.

Aftermath of the terrible crash at Moorgate. (©TfL from the London Transport Museum collection)

After a lengthy inquest, the coroner ruled the incident to have been a case of accidental death, but the true reality of what actually happened is still something of a mystery today. A concerned public and the families of the victims all wanted answers. There had been no apparent fault with either the train or trackside equipment, and therefore the attention inevitably turned to Leslie Newson.

One school of thought is that Newson may have intentionally caused the incident, perhaps as part of an elaborate suicide. It was a theory given substantial weight at the time due to the testimony of witnesses. Some survivors on board claimed that they remembered feeling the train accelerate as it pulled into the station. Witnesses on the platform suggested that Newson was either seated or standing, and looking directly forward just before impact. Accounts such as this were consistent with post-mortem results that showed the driver to have been holding on to the controls at the point of impact.

They were accusations that deeply offended the friends and family of Newson. It was pointed out that he had shown no signs of being either depressed or suicidal. In fact, much was made of how a quantity of money found in Newson's pocket was said to be for a car he was planning to buy his daughter later in the day.

Others believe instead that Newson had suffered a sudden medical condition which may have caused temporary amnesia or paralysis. It would still be consistent with the witness accounts from the platform, and it is certainly a theory that is kinder to the memory of Newson and everyone else that lost their lives. There was no indication from the post-mortem that the cause may have been either a heart attack or a stroke.

No one will ever know the full truth, but in 1975 it was enough to knock the confidence of passengers. It was a testing time for the London Underground, and for motormen across every line. There had been safety concerns over stations with dead-end stops like the one at Moorgate for several years. Motorman deaths had occurred due to accidental overruns at Edgware in 1946, Tooting Broadway in 1971 and at Rayners Lane in 1972, and there had also been non-fatal incidents at Aldwych station (now disused). After Moorgate, it was clear that changes would finally need to be made.

There have also been a number of other incidents attributed to the fault of individual staff members, some of which caused death and serious injury. In 1938, a wiring error by an engineer resulted in a signal failure

The location of the Moorgate disaster as it looks today. (Author)

that caused a deadly crash on the District line, killing six people. Loss of control or a lapse in concentration were also the causes of smaller incidents on the Central line in the early 1980s, and there was also a collision in thick fog at Kilburn station on the Jubilee line in 1984 that resulted in the death of the motorman.

FIRE AT KING'S CROSS

The blame for some incidents can sometimes go way beyond the actions of just one person, however. The problem can sometimes be the result of systematic failings across an entire organisation, and it's this problem that is widely accepted to have been a major contributing factor to the King's Cross fire disaster of 1987.

In a time where health and safety now governs every aspect of public life, and where smoking is not permitted inside any public building, it's hard to imagine that passengers were able to smoke on the London Underground as recently as the mid-1980s.

It had long been a concern on the system, particularly as many station escalators included wooden steps and skirting, and there were also wooden handrails and other such features elsewhere. The London Underground were slow to implement smoking bans, however, no doubt weary of the impact it could have on passenger numbers. It was only after fires at Goodge Street station in 1981 and Oxford Circus station in 1984 that smoking was finally banned on trains and partially banned from stations.

The London fire brigade had for several years been advising the London Underground to abolish a strict policy in place that dictated how station staff must attempt to deal with a fire before calling the brigade. The recommendations were ignored, and it would prove to be one of several errors of judgement during the King's Cross fire.

The chain of events began on the evening of 18 November, when a small fire close to the Victoria line platforms was extinguished by a member of the station staff. A short time later, a Piccadilly line passenger discarded a match on an escalator. The match, almost certainly used to light a cigarette, fell inside the mechanism of the escalator, which had not been cleaned for several months. Litter and dust provided fuel for the burning match, and a small fire soon ignited. The amount of wood surrounding the fire ensured that it spread fast.

At this point a series of mistakes were made. Passengers alerted station staff to the fire, but they proceeded to investigate the wrong escalators. In accordance with the guidelines requiring staff to attempt to extinguish fires, when the correct escalator was inspected, a lack of a visible flame led the staff members to believe there was no actual fire.

The emergency services were therefore not alerted, and no alarm calls or warnings were sent to the various control rooms across the system. Trains continued to arrive at the station as a result, with passengers alighting unaware there was a fire. The apparent lack of any real concern also led to no sprinkler system or extinguishers being activated.

Within twenty minutes of the fire starting it had developed into a deadly blaze. When it was finally extinguished there were thirty-one people dead and dozens more injured. As with the accident at Moorgate, the media, passengers and politicians all wanted to know how this could have happened. It was another major blow for the London Underground's reputation, and to the integrity of safety.

Memorial to the victims of the King's Cross fire. (Author)

CALL FOR INSPECTOR SANDS

There are several code names used by London Underground staff as a way of describing incidents without causing alarm to passengers. Most go unnoticed when heard on public address announcements in a station, but one particular code name that passengers have picked up on is 'Inspector Sands'. Said to have originated in the theatre industry, it tends to be heard on the Underground when a fire alarm has been activated.

ALL CHANGE

The devastating impact of the disasters at Moorgate and King's Cross led to several changes within the company, including how the highest-ranked staff members organised their railway, and how drivers and station staff worked on a daily basis.

The crash at Moorgate resulted in faster implementation of new measures that were already being rolled out in the wake of the previous dead-end incidents. For any station with such a layout, a new system was installed that made better use of warning signals and automatic train-stop devices.

Conclusions drawn from the King's Cross fire would have an even greater impact. Firstly, smoking was now fully banned across the entire system. A damning report into the disaster concluded that the London Underground had for many years disregarded fire safety as a priority.

It was now the organisation's number one concern, and all station staff were fully trained in how to act in an emergency situation. Better communication with the emergency services was also implemented, including an end to the previous policy of only contacting the fire brigade as a last resort.

The enquiry also prompted London Underground to begin long-overdue upgrade work. Wooden escalators and fittings were removed from almost all stations. Many ticket halls were also renovated, and machinery and equipment would now be cleaned and serviced regularly.

Note that the platform where the Moorgate crash took place can still be seen today, in the National Rail section of the station. There is a plaque in the ticket hall at King's Cross St Pancras station dedicated to the memory of those who died.

NEW TERROR

The various safety and institutional changes have undoubtedly saved lives since, and have restored people's faith in a system that in actual fact has a near-impeccable safety record. It was also because of these changes that London Underground's station staff and train operators were so well prepared for the tragic events that unfolded on 7 July 2005.

The terrorist attacks that were quickly dubbed 7/7 caused mass devastation across the city, just hours after London had been awarded the 2012 Olympic Games. Because the attacks were concentrated on London's underground railway, they made many hundreds of thousands of people potential victims. By the time the onslaught was over there were fifty-six people dead, including the four suicide bombers.

Bombs had been detonated on two Circle line trains and one on the Piccadilly line. The terrorists also planned a fourth bomb, this time on the Northern line, but it failed to detonate (it exploded on a bus later in the day, causing further deaths).

By 9.30 a.m. parts of the Tube network resembled a war zone. Thousands were trapped inside deep-level tunnels, and there were dead or injured passengers on the impacted trains. London Underground staff were quick to respond, and put into practice their trained skills.

Train operators and station staff descended into the darkness to assist with injuries and evacuate passengers by guiding them through smoke-filled tunnels, and out to safety via stations and other emergency exits. More than 250,000 passengers were successfully evacuated, saving many lives and helping to ease the fears of confused and panic-stricken Londoners.

NEW TRIUMPH

The day of 7 July 2005 is one that no one working on the London Underground is likely to forget, but their hard work and ability to remain calm under such pressure was recognised by all. The disaster had a direct link to the 2012 Olympic Games, coming a day after London won the right to host them. It made the Games themselves even more poignant, and once again it was the skill and preparedness of staff that helped ensure they were a success.

In the months leading up to the start of the Games, held in July and August 2012, Londoners had been predicting meltdown on the Tube system. In reality, as soon as they began it became clear that the expected chaos would not materialise. The Jubilee line and the Docklands Light Railway – the parts of the system set to be used most during the Games – managed to handle the extra strain with relative ease. Elsewhere, advanced communication, good signage, effective passenger flow, clear train operator announcements and helpful station staff made sure that there was little incident.

The 2012 Games are widely considered to have been a major triumph, and even the most cynical TfL customers would find it hard to deny that this was thanks in part to London's 150-year-old underground railway.

ACKNOWLEDGEMENTS

Thanks as always to my amazing wife Louise Pedroche for giving me so much support during the time it took to write this book, and for providing the many great photographs. I would also like to thank my family and friends, and everybody at the London Transport Museum. I am grateful for those who shared with me their knowledge of working for the London Underground, including Eric Stuart, Jim Bleasdale, Brian Parker and Daniel Newberry. Last but not least, thanks to Chrissy McMorris and everyone else at The History Press.

REFERENCES AND FURTHER READING

SELECTED BOOKS

Ackroyd, P., *London Under* (Vintage, 2012).

Bayman, B., *Underground Official Handbook* (Capital Transport, 2008).

Bownes, D., Green, O. & Mullins, S., *Underground: How the Tube Shaped London* (Allen Lane, 2012).

Bruce, J. Graeme & Croome, D.F., *The Twopenny Tube* (Capital Transport, 1996).

Bruce, J. Graeme, *The Big Tube: A Short Illustrated History of London's Great Northern & City Railway* (London Transport, 1976).

Connor, J.E., *London's Disused Underground Stations* (Capital Transport, 2006).

Croome, D.F., *The Piccadilly Line* (Capital Transport, 1998).

Emmerson, A., *The London Underground* (Shire Library, 2010).

Emmerson, A., *The Underground Pioneers* (Capital Transport, 2000).

Garbutt, P.E., *How the Underground Works* (London Transport, 1963).

Griffiths, R., *Mind The Doors!* (Silver Link Publishing, 2002).

Horne, M., *The Bakerloo Line* (Capital Transport, 2001).

Horne, M., *The Northern Line* (Capital Transport, 2009).

Horne, M., *The Victoria Line* (Capital Transport, 2004).

Jones, R., *London's Transport: A Popular History* (Ian Allan, 2008).

Lee, C., *The Metropolitan Line: A Brief History* (London Transport, 1972).

Martin, A., *Underground Overground: A Passenger's History of the Tube* (Profile Books Ltd, 2012).

Mathewson, A., Laval, D., Elton, J., Kentley, E. & Hulse, R., *The Brunel Tunnel* (The Brunel Museum, 2006).

Pearce, A., Hardy, B. & Stannard, C., *Docklands Light Railway Official Handbook* (Capital Transport, 2006).

Powell, K., *The Jubilee Line Extension* (Laurence King Publishing, 2000).

Rotondaro, A., *Women at Work on London's Transport* (Tempus Publishing, 2004).

Smith, S., *Underground London* (Abacus, 2004).

Taylor, C., *Londoners* (Granta, 2011).

Wolmar, C., *The Subterranean Railway* (Atlantic Books, 2004).

SELECTED PUBLICATIONS

A Century of Tunnelling and Where We Go Now (British Tunnelling Society, 2000).

Underground News (London Underground Railway Society, various issues).

'The Waterloo and City Railway: A Visit to the Works' (*The Graphic*, November 1895).

SELECTED WEBSITES

Note that these websites were all available at the time of publication, but may have since lapsed.

http://www.20thcenturylondon.org.uk/
http://www.britishpathe.com/
http://www.crossrail.co.uk/
http://districtdave.proboards.com/
http://www.geograph.org.uk/
http://www.ianvisits.co.uk/
http://www.londonist.com/
http://www.londonreconnections.com/
http://www.london-underground.blogspot.co.uk/
http://www.ltmcollection.org/
http://www.lurs.org.uk/
http://www.trainweb.org/tubeprune/
http://www.tubelines.com/

SELECTED TV PROGRAMMES, FILMS AND DVDS

Fluffies (British Pathé, 1944)
London on the Move (British Film Institute, 2012)
The Tube (BBC/Blast! Films, 2012)

INDEX